ON POINT

To Sarah —

Hope This inspires
a song or two! :)

Keep abating! Sarah!

All best,
Tracy

ON POINT

A Guide to Writing the Military Story

TRACY CROW

POTOMAC BOOKS

An imprint of the
University of Nebraska Press

Library of Congress Cataloging-in-
Publication Data
Crow, Tracy.
On point: a guide to writing the
military story / Tracy Crow.
pages   cm
ISBN 978-1-61234-709-7 (pbk.: alk. paper)
ISBN 978-1-61234-777-6 (epub)
ISBN 978-1-61234-778-3 (mobi)
ISBN 978-1-61234-779-0 (pdf)
1. Autobiography—Authorship.
2. Military biography. 3. Biography as
a literary form. 4. Soldiers' writings—
United States—Biography—History
and criticism. I. Title.
CT25.C76 2015
355.0092—dc23
2015015470

Set in Scala Sans by L. Auten.

In memory of Marine Corps Chief Warrant Officer N.H.N.

In a world of lies and liars, an honest work of art is always an act of social responsibility. —ROBERT MCKEE

Contents

Preface   xi

Acknowledgments   xv

1. Owning the Story of Our Lives   1

2. Discovering Where the Small Fires Burn   23

3. Embracing the Writer (and Process) Within   41

4. Plotting Our Stories with Timelines,
   Memories, Outcomes   55

5. Developing Characters, Conflicts,
   and Connections   69

6. Shaping Our Storytelling with Structure   87

7. Activating Energy Shifts within Our Scenes   107

8. Sharing Our Stories—When and How   115

9. Navigating the World of Publishing   123

10. Gifting Ourselves with a Writing Life   131

Additional Resources   135

Preface

Several years ago I prefaced my memoir, *Eyes Right: Confessions from a Woman Marine*, with these words: "Every Marine has a story." Since the memoir's release, I've had the privilege of reading and listening to many stories from veterans of all ranks and services—stories ranging from humorous to heartrending and from World War II to the present. What surprised me most, however, were the military stories I hadn't expected—those from the families of military veterans. Through stories shared by parents, spouses, significant others, close friends, and grown children and grandchildren, I learned how the cross-generational impact of military traditions and customs, leadership values, long absences, psychological and physical wounds, and tragic combat and training deaths have shaped their lives and in many cases continue to do so.

At the heart of all those stories, whether shared by a veteran or a family member, appeared a yearning for deeper understanding. I believe writing about our military experiences can lead us to that deeper awareness of self and of our place in this world. My hope is that *On Point* will serve as a guide.

A few words about the title. *On point*, or *taking point*, is a military term used to describe the infantryman who will lead an often dangerous patrol. To be on point is to place one's life in the riskiest of all positions. So risky, in fact, that the point position is rotated from patrol to patrol. Writing is risky, too. In revisiting memories, I have keenly recalled the risk. As notable memoirist Patricia Hampl claims, "To write one's life is to live it twice." Revisiting my past over and over again during the writing and revision process of my memoir was nearly more than I could bear at times. But writing the memoir provided a much deeper self-awareness about the controversial events that surrounded the end of my military career and the rocky transition to civilian life.

After the release of the memoir, and while the idea of *On Point* was floating in and out of consciousness, I lost a dear friend. A gifted storyteller, he was also a former Marine and the son of a Marine who had survived combat in the Pacific during World War II. But after returning from Beirut, my friend, like far too many of our veterans, became so disillusioned with civilian life and with himself that he ended his life with a gunshot. In the wake of his mental suffering and suicide, he left two teenaged daughters and a slew of Marine friends wondering how we had missed the signs. What, if anything, we asked, could we have said that would have made a difference? Maybe nothing; maybe something.

What I know for certain is that our friend would have loved the motivations and intentions behind this book—*and* that I finally yielded to *On Point*'s refusal to be shaped like any other classic college textbook on writing. From the outset *On Point* seemed determined to grow organically from roots in part memoir, part meditations and musings, and part writing maxims. *Just call it a damn conversation, for crying out loud,* our Marine friend, who was also a former journalist, would have succinctly and bluntly put it. It's not an exaggeration to say this book in many ways was born out of grief over losing him and his storytelling gifts.

My wish is for *On Point* to inspire you to write about your military experiences and, more important, to grant you permission. Your story matters, even if you don't yet fully believe so. But *On Point* cannot and should not be used as a replacement for post-traumatic stress disorder (PTSD) cognitive therapy or therapy related to treatment for moral injury. As you read and engage the twenty-six *On Point* writing projects, I urge you to take care of yourself by monitoring your feelings and reactions to memories and by discussing them with your health professional, loved ones, or trusted friends.

Of course, I'm also anticipating your military mind-set of "see the hill, take the hill." You'll be tempted, as would I, to read through this entire book, skipping the writing projects until the end, as if this book were the required text for a course on speed reading.

Please don't. Challenge yourself to complete each writing project before moving on to the next project or the next chapter. Trust the process. This writing thing you're considering? It's a gift you're giving yourself.

Acknowledgments

After the suicide of a Marine Corps friend, the idea for this book began to take form and then grew, as with other writing projects, from conversations with fellow veterans and writers who have for many years supported my life as a writer.

No one, however, has been more supportive than Jeffery Hess, a Navy veteran, military writer, founder, and leader of the DD-214 Writers' Workshop for veterans in Tampa, Florida, and editor of two awarding-winning volumes of military fiction. Thank you, dear friend.

I'd also like to thank friends and fellow writers David Abrams, Pinckney Benedict, Caleb S. Cage, Dario DiBattista, Jessica Handler, Kevin Jones, Brooke King, Fred Leebron, Lorrie Lykins, Margaret MacInnis, Rebecca McClanahan, Dinty W. Moore, Donald Morrill, Thomas Vincent Nowaczyk, Libby Oberg, Kathryn Rhett, CJ Scarlet, Michael Steinberg, Kathryn Trueblood, Helen and Peter Wallace, and Sterling Watson.

To my editor, Bridget Barry, special thanks for believing in the idea of this book long before I'd written the first word; and to Sam Dorrance and the entire team at the University of Nebraska Press / Potomac Books: your tireless, devoted commitment toward quality uplifts me and allows me to sleep at night.

Deep gratitude goes out to the many former colleagues and students at the University of Tampa, Eckerd College, and Queens University of Charlotte who continue to offer all sorts of support.

Lastly, what would I be without family? For you especially—Polly, Vern, Mike, Morgan, Brian, and Mark—thank you for sustaining me with unconditional encouragement and love.

ON POINT

1

Owning the Story of Our Lives

Owning our story can be hard but not nearly as difficult as spending our lives running from it. —DR. BRENÉ BROWN

When I left the Marines in 1987, after nearly ten years, I left with a story I never intended to tell.

That all changed. Eventually, I would share my story, even though it was rife with admissions of guilt and shame and regret and finally, after many years of consternation and denial, compassion for that younger version of myself. I have now told *her* story, and many other stories since, because when I was ten, I dreamed of becoming a writer.

What I couldn't have known at ten is that a flip decision to join the Marines in an effort to escape a childhood home filled with domestic violence and to save myself from teenage alcoholism would become the vehicle for driving me toward a future writing life. Had I known then that I was facing *forty-two* more years before the publication of my first book, which, as it turns out, was the memoir about my life as a Marine, I might have ditched the whole writing plan I had as a kid for Plan B. Plan B was to become a professional dog handler, satisfying my second greatest passion. By now I could be judging best in show for the Westminster Kennel Club.

But in 1969, at ten, I was willing myself toward a writing life and still living in the last home my family would share before the divorce that tore us asunder. Our home in Roanoke, Virginia, was a rented 1940s Craftsman bungalow with a wide front porch and a living room full of books. Roanoke is a picturesque valley town surrounded by the Appalachians in the southwest corner of the state. Every night an electronically lit star atop Mill Mountain flashed red if someone had died that day in a traffic accident; if all in Roanoke were spared such a tragedy, the star shone a brilliant white. Every night thousands and thousands of pairs of eyes, including mine, turned toward the mountaintop for the news of the day. An early form of social media, you might say, because a red star sighting prompted hundreds of telephone calls throughout the valley. Had our family still been together and in Roanoke ten years later, when my father died in a fiery crash, the blazing red star would have felt even more injurious.

Our little bungalow, the first home to house my dream of becoming a writer, sat impressively atop a steep hill and overlooked a busy two-lane road that truckers used as a shortcut to the interstate. In the dense woods that nearly enveloped the house, my younger brother and I played army and stealthily sneaked down a dirt path that led to the main road so we could spy on high school kids who used our old path as a lovers' lane. The idea was to scare the daylights out of anyone we found parked on our property.

To reach our house at the top of the hill, we had to climb a steep, S-shaped, asphalt driveway. During winter the driveway provided a somewhat perilous sledding opportunity. Our favorite sled was shaped like a small satellite TV dish, and we'd grab the canvas handles and hang on for dear life as we bounded down the hill, leaning into the curves, brakeless, preparing our bodies for a final ditch from the sled before reaching the creek that was too powerful for even Mother Nature to freeze.

During summers my brother and I traipsed through that creek, searching for tadpoles and frogs and leaping from snakes. In the field below our driveway and near the creek, we played baseball during the summer for hours and hours with the kids who lived on the hill above us. Their dad, Carroll, was our landlord. I thought it was spelled *Carol*, and I spent an inordinate amount of imagination on a man whose parents would give him a girl's name.

By the time I was ten, we had lived in four other homes. I only have snatches of memories from those. But the bungalow at the top of that hill . . . the bungalow that couldn't begin to house my father's anger but could house all the books I ever wanted to read at ten . . . was the first and last home of my childhood. By thirteen we had moved again, and this time separation from my abusive, alcoholic father meant separation, too, from all those lovely books.

Nothing remains the same. Today the old road to our Roanoke home has been widened to four lanes. Highway engineers surgically sliced into the hill. The bungalow has disappeared, and so has Carroll's home. Not a trace of my family's old life there exists anywhere but in my memory. And I go there often, for that is where I discovered my love for reading and writing. Both were an escape from the realities associated with life inside a home filled with domestic violence, though I couldn't have articulated that at the time. My father's alcoholism, most likely a self-medicated attempt to wrestle manic depression, left holes in Sheetrock from doors flung too wide open, ripped long gashes in the cheap kitchen linoleum from his chair pushed too violently from the table in mad attempts to escape the loud sounds of our chewing, and left permanent scars on our hearts and psyches.

The upside of my childhood, however, was that my parents loved to read. They filled the built-in shelves with books. Every birthday and holiday delivered more and more books. I devoured them all, even the ones my parents thought I wasn't old enough to read tucked away in drawers. I read and reread them all, especially Louisa May Alcott's *Little Women*. I dreamed of becoming Josephine, brave Jo, unafraid to speak her mind and unafraid to express imagination through the written art of storytelling during a time when women were often locked away as hysterical if they insisted on writing poems and stories. By the time I was twelve, in 1971, I had reread *Little Women* more than a dozen times, each time discovering an overlooked nuance. I needed a hero in those days. Josephine March became mine in much the same way, I suppose, Harry Potter and his friends have become heroes to another generation.

I had no idea how I would become a writer or what becoming a writer actually meant, other than lots of hard work, surely, associated with getting all the right words in just the right order, and of course, since my vision of writing was formed by Alcott's fictional, defiant

Josephine March, enduring long, lovely stretches of loneliness. Still, I wanted to become a writer. Around the sixth grade I drafted my first serious short story, "Beyond the Basement Door," inspired by our creepy, dank basement with the dirt floor. I only crawled down those rickety steps once. Once was enough. No doubt my short story about the basement was melodramatic and terribly flawed, but my classmates and teacher cheered me on. I can't remember anything about the story now other than the title and the way it felt to affect others with my words.

A few months later I found myself the unlikely voice of a protest against the elementary school's ridiculous no-pants dress code for girls. My classmates and I were fed up with standing around bus stops during blustery, wintry days and trudging through snow in drifts above our knees with no more protection than our silly kneesocks. We demanded the right to wear pants during the winter. After meeting with the male principal, who reluctantly agreed with our petition after hearing my argument, my teacher, Mrs. Cochran, pulled me aside and said that I should become a lawyer. "You certainly know how to argue," she'd said.

"But I'm supposed to be a writer." I felt myself slip-sliding into melancholy on the long walk back to our classroom because Mrs. Cochran no longer saw me for the writer I believed I was preordained to become.

Soon after my parents' divorce hurled us all toward a new state of madness, my father got in trouble with loan sharks and moved back in with his parents in Greensboro, North Carolina; my mother had to work two jobs, and the stress nearly broke her spirit and mine; my brother landed in one juvenile home after another; and I began to drink, starting at fifteen, shortly after the night our neighbor shot himself in the head. I had been babysitting his two children and had barely closed the front door of our post-divorce duplex, attached to his, when I heard the explosion, followed by his wife's bloodcurdling screams. The man who had just pressed a twenty-dollar bill into my hand, winked, and thanked me for putting his children to bed had raised a pistol to his temple and shot himself dead. The bullet nearly came through the Sheetrock, and had it wormed its way through, it would have struck me as well, just as I was standing in our tiny foyer, turning the lock on our front door. In the hours and days that followed, I remember thinking the whole world had gone mad, including the world that centered around my father, and worried about whether madness could be transferred from one person to another as simply as, say, a lingering staph germ on a twenty-dollar bill.

So, I started drinking. I suppose, like my father, I was trying to self-medicate. For a few years I just felt numb. A little crazy and numb at the same time, if that's possible. That's how I see it now, looking back. I didn't believe I belonged in college or deserved a college experience, so I joined the Marines, mostly as a way to overcome my alcoholism and to escape an inappropriate relationship with my boss.

You see, everyone has a reason for joining the Marines, or whatever branch of the military they join. Maybe joining the military is a way to pay homage to a family steeped in military tradition. Maybe joining is an opportunity to leave a small town with small minds and small job options. Maybe joining is a way to pay for college. Regardless, everyone has a reason—and a narrative they tell to justify the reason.

Everyone has a story, I firmly believe. You're reading this because you believe you have at least one story within you that needs to be released. You're just not sure how to release it or whether you *should* release it. I get that. Remember, I'm the one with the story I never intended to tell anyone, especially my daughter, who was only seven when I left the Marines.

Maybe you're wrestling with something from your military past, something from long ago. Maybe you're one of the thousands enrolled this minute under the best GI Bill in history and struggling with how to share the story that's rising with an intensity so excessive you nearly choke on it. But there you are in a college classroom, the oldest freshman, and fighting the urge not to beat up the kid who won't stop complaining—I'm talking seriously life-and-death complaining—about the canceled Frisbee tournament in the Quad. I get that too. I was a college professor for nine years, and while I loved my students and the opportunity to shape young minds, the former Marine side of me often wished I could snatch a few by the collar and remind them of young people like you, like me—the ones who fought internal and external wars for those who elected to opt out of military service. I found myself, too, choking back retorts to fellow professors who were rich with morality and political ideology and who would never fully understand the world the way that you and I understand it.

So, maybe you're sitting there in class, simmering to a boil when a misguided professor outs your veteran status to the class because you believe you have the right to choose the moment when, and with whom for that matter, you'll share this information and because you want to avoid the obvious, stupid questions from the naive nineteen-year-olds: *What was it like over there?* And of course, *Did you ever kill anyone?* For fifteen years after the end of my life as a Marine, I lied whenever someone asked why I'd left the Corps; the truth would have embarrassed us both.

If you are enrolled at a college, I hope you're familiar with Student Veterans of America (sva), a national organization with chapters at colleges and universities around the country. If sva hasn't opened a chapter at your school, I encourage you to contact the organization for assistance (you'll find contact information in the Additional Resources section at the end of *On Point*—there you will also find recommendations for further military reading and my favorite writing craft books as well as writing shortcut tips and a sample email query letter for agents).

Maybe you're reading this because you're a concerned professor who is actively searching for a way to better support the sudden influx of military veteran students in your classroom. Thank you.

Or maybe you're someone who's beginning to believe what they say about how writing helps you discover who you really are. Socrates claimed the unexamined life isn't worth living. Neither is the unlived life worth examining. But that's not your problem. If you've served in the military—directly or indirectly as a parent, spouse, or child of a military service member—you've lived plenty.

From the day Kathleen M. Rodgers married an Air Force fighter pilot, her goal was to bring about awareness of military subjects. "The publishing world likes to categorize subject matter," says the award-winning author of *The Final Salute* and *Johnny Come Lately*, "and they sometimes refer to military themed stories as belonging to a niche market. But there's nothing 'niche' about being human. Whether military or civilian, we all have similar hopes, fears, and dreams for those we love and for ourselves."

Writing about your military experiences, even if you decide to turn your true stories into fiction, will help you develop a deeper understanding about your life, your decisions, and the motives behind your decisions because meaningful writing comes from identifying meaningful patterns. Meaningful writing requires a self-awakening. When we write, we're training ourselves to search deeply for motive behind choices, whether we're writing about ourselves in a memoir or essay or about the characters within our military short story or novel.

Maybe you've turned to *On Point* to test the theory you've heard too often about how writing can't be taught. I can easily, happily, dispel this theory. I am a product of writing instruction that began during my early years as a Marine Corps journalist. I entered that job with no more knowledge about writing than how to tell a complete sentence from a fragment. Every article I wrote for the base newspaper came back redlined so heavily I couldn't make out my own words beneath the sea of red. My master gunnery sergeant (E-9) would prowl in front of my desk as I typed draft after draft—a yardstick beating against the side of his leg like a metronome. Occasionally, he'd whack the top of my desk with the yardstick to rush me toward deadline. One day I turned in an article about a lance corporal (E-3) who made miniature weapons that actually fired. I saw the master gunnery sergeant headed my way and braced myself for the wave of corrections. He dropped the article on my desk, and I saw a single red mark to indicate a missed comma. That's all. A single missed comma. I was speechless. He wasn't, however. "You're finally more than a good-looking pair of legs," he said, and walked away, striking the side of his leg with that damn yardstick.

Certainly, a solid understanding of grammar and syntax is important, and if you sense your skills are rusty, I encourage you to review the resource recommendations at the end of this book. But when I'm talking about the teaching of writing and the art of writing, I'm referring to the act of *storytelling*. And that's what the master gunnery sergeant was teaching me: how to tell a story. Just because some of us have a more solid grasp of the English language doesn't mean we know how to convey a story on the page for readers, and this inability to transfer onto the page exactly what our mind sees can be frustrating enough to turn off new writers. Please know that if this is your fear, you are not alone. Noted nineteenth-century novelist Gustave Flaubert said: "I am irritated by my own writing. I am like a violinist whose ear is true, but whose fingers refuse to reproduce precisely the sound he hears within."

All writers share this frustration from time to time. But rest assured that writing can be taught. Let me demystify the whole process of writing right here. Writers—just like painters, musicians, sculptors, and any other type of artist—employ a set of skills, and these skills are learned and honed over time. We're not born, for example, knowing the musical scales or where they fall on a piano keyboard any more than we're born with the skills for writing a conversation between two characters in a short story. We learn how through a number of ways: by reading and by having our own work corrected by skilled instructors. We're not born knowing how to create interesting characters and interesting dilemmas that will engage our readers from the first page to the last. We learn how to do this by reading voraciously and by submitting our own work through a critique process that highlights what's working and what's not.

Are there writing prodigies just as there are music or artist prodigies? Possibly. If so, I believe it's because their brains are capable of absorbing more sensory detail about the writing process than the rest of us. Maybe the language part of their brains is overdeveloped. Who knows? What I do know for certain is that we can be taught specific writing skills. Sure, we'll have to practice these skills in every story we attempt to tell about ourselves and our military experiences, just as an aspiring pianist must practice the scales over and over. Eventually, however, we'll be writing without thinking much about how to punctuate a line of dialogue or whether our pacing through a plot is too fast or too slow. Instead, our writing minds will eventually expand beyond these basics and into skills such as how to make meaningful connections in our work and how to enhance themes regarding personal sacrifice, joy, grief, vulnerability, shame, loss, and surrender that shine a light on the human condition.

Are some writers better than others? Absolutely. I read great work all the time, and for a moment—just a moment—I confess I wonder why I even bother to craft another sentence. And then I snap out of it. After all, nobody can write the way I do. And nobody will write the way *you* write. Every writer has a unique voice on the page. If you doubt this, open three books you have lying around. Read aloud the opening paragraphs for each. Do they sound alike? I bet they don't. Why? Because every writer has a unique voice, which is determined by the writer's use of vocabulary, sentence and paragraph constructions, and use of language that evokes the five senses of sight, sound, smell, touch, and taste. You have a voice right now, and soon your writer's voice will find its way onto the page and into the hearts and minds of other readers.

Recently, I stumbled across a video of a creative writing professor at Florida State University who was brave enough to allow the videotaping of his writing process for a short story. I say brave because the process, even for this successful writing professor, is not a pretty one. It goes something like this: write a sentence; delete that sentence; rewrite that sentence with a slight variation; delete again; rewrite again with a stronger variation from the earlier attempts; write another sentence; *wish* to delete it but take a leap of faith and continue to a third and then a fourth; then delete sentence 3 and revise sentence 4. See what I mean? The artistic process can be a messy one for even the most accomplished writer, but so is the artistic process for those creating a musical composition or a painting.

My goal here is to arm you with an array of writing tools so that you'll feel confident enough to begin the storytelling process of your military experiences. I've written the book I wish had been available when I began to write about mine. In 2002 plenty of solid writing craft books existed, and plenty more have been published since. I've included a list of my favorites and those I've assigned as textbooks to my college students at the end of this book. But not one specifically addressed the complexities of writing the military story.

The idea of crafting this book simultaneously thrilled and terrified me. My first thought was, *Who do you think you are that you can tell others how to write their military stories?* I began to rationalize: I've published an award-winning memoir about my life as a Marine in the 1980s; published a successfully selling military novel under my pen name, Carver Greene; compiled and edited a volume of military nonfiction; edited nonfiction for a literary journal; taught creative writing and journalism for nine years at two colleges; and, oh yeah, spent ten years as a journalist in the Marine Corps.

I wasn't sure any or all of this qualified me to write this sort of book, but I was willing to try. Trying meant immersing myself in research. I started with studies by James W. Pennebaker regarding the therapeutic benefits of writing, and I read other studies about the specific effects of writing on post-traumatic stress. I also spoke with veterans such as Brooke King, a soldier who served in Iraq and who suffers from post-traumatic stress. King was willing to share how writing has helped her. "It helps to make sense of what is happening to you," she said. "In cognitive processing therapy a veteran with PTSD is asked to confront their traumas head-on by writing down the incident, and then connect the feeling associated with it. I didn't think writing was helping at first, but I kept doing it because it was the only way I knew how to express myself."

Over time, she said, the nightmares decreased and the feelings of guilt and shame lessened. "I began to understand that surviving the war was a blessing and not a curse."

Today King is the author of a chapbook of poetry about her war experiences. Additionally, she has published a short story in the military anthology *Home of the Brave: Somewhere in the Sand* and in my anthology, *Red, White, and True: Stories from Veterans and Families, World War II to Present.*

Another veteran who discovered benefits from writing about his military experience is former Marine Thomas Vincent Nowaczyk. He participated in a PTSD program provided by a North Chicago VA facility. "That program really showed me the power of writing when it comes to confronting and exorcising horrific traumatic events. It's a different sort of writing, to empty the emotional locker so to speak, but the stuff that comes out is strong and powerful."

For Nowaczyk, who has now published a military short story as well as an essay about the experience that initiated his PTSD, all the things he had internalized for years finally lost their emotional charge after he put them on paper, including the feelings surrounding the violent suicides of two friends. "The writing is hard work, mind numbing and emotionally draining," he said. "It is the peace you gain at the end that makes the effort worthwhile."

Writing may also benefit those who are suffering with moral injury, which has been dubbed "inner conflict" by some health professionals. As David Wood so aptly describes in his *Huffington Post* exposé, "[Moral injury] is a violation of the sense of right and wrong that leaves a wound on the soul." We're taught a moral code in basic training, but what happens when a decision we make under duress or under orders produces horrible results—the killing of innocent civilians, for example? We're only just now beginning to understand the depth of moral injury. While the sufferer of PTSD lives under a hypervigilant state of awareness that is often agitated by sounds and smells, moral injury sufferers are quietly consumed with feelings of shame, guilt, and worthlessness.

Also in preparation for this book, I added more military literature titles to my reading experience and bookshelves (see the recommended reading list at the end of this book). And I interviewed a number of veterans who are today's emerging military writers, editors, and veterans writing workshop leaders and included their experiences here. I spoke with a handful of today's top creative writing faculty who are working, or have worked, with military veterans in their classrooms; their input has mostly been included as background, though several have allowed me to quote them directly.

Look, not everyone has a desire to publish. You may not be inter-ested in sharing your military stories outside of your immediate fam-ily, though you're beginning, perhaps, to realize you have memories you'd like to record and preserve for yourself, your children, and your grandchildren. You might even be thinking that no one outside your family is likely to find your military experience interesting enough to read, anyway, because you didn't experience combat or return home severely changed—emotionally or physically—from a deployment in the Middle East or beat down thoughts of suicide or receive a medal for heroism. Actually, those who win combat medals are usually the least likely to tell their stories, for many reasons, including those that writing may actually help.

It's a natural association to assume a military story equals a story about war. Not so. My military experience during the 1980s, for exam-ple, didn't include combat. A few months before the 2012 release of *Eyes Right*, I started a blog that I named *First Marine Moms*, and I solicited stories from other women who, like me, had been among that generation of women Marines who were the first to be moms while being Marines. You see, before our generation the Depart-ment of Defense immediately discharged pregnant service mem-bers. This meant that all the women who came before us had been compelled to choose between motherhood and military career. That is, until a group of women lobbied Congress. So, there we were, the first pregnant Marines, standing, often too long, in formation, being forced to run physical fitness tests much too far into our pregnan-cies, and dealing for the first time in the history of the Corps with calls from child day cares regarding earaches, colds, broken bones, and the like.

Not surprisingly, we weren't totally accepted, especially by our women leaders who had passed on their biological opportunities for motherhood. In *Eyes Right* I could only tell my story and hope in the end that my story adequately represented the story of a generation. But I wanted to hear from others, and this is why I initiated the blog. I was astounded. Not one of these women, like me, had ever expe-rienced combat, for this was the 1980s, a relatively quiet era of the

Cold War, notwithstanding the Beirut bombing, the Grenada invasion, and apprehensions about Manuel Noriega in Nicaragua, yet each had a compelling story about her experience as a pregnant woman in the Marine Corps. Each woman expressed her gratitude for having been given a platform on my blog for sharing her story. Their children, in most cases, and even their husbands hadn't known the full story of what they had endured as that first generation of pregnant women Marines.

Your military story, like mine, probably includes a rich amount of mundane and humorous material—the sort of material that can still provide our readers with insights into who we were during those years and how those events shaped who we are today. Remember that boot camp bunk mate from Wisconsin? The one with the funny last name that became a bull's-eye target for drill instructors? How about the unrelenting sand fleas at Parris Island? What about all those crazy antics among bored sailors at sea? Shore leave in the Far East? Oktoberfest in Germany? One of my former college students told our class that she and her family hadn't discovered until after her grandfather's death that he'd received not one but two Purple Hearts—a discovery that deepened the family's appreciation and curiosity and saddened them that they would never know the story behind the second Purple Heart. Are you, or have you been, a military spouse? If so, then you have stories about the cross-country and overseas moves you've made, the children's fears you've soothed, and the ordeals associated with the Murphy's Law breakdown of car, refrigerator, washing machine, and anything else in your home with a motor that happened as soon as your military guy or gal shipped out.

I love this opening scene depicting the resilience of a military wife and mother by Rebecca McClanahan, daughter of a Marine Corps officer, that appears in her essay "Dependent," excerpted from her collection of essays, *The Riddle Song and Other Rememberings*:

> In one of my earliest memories, my mother is standing on an unpacked crate beneath the ceiling of a Quonset hut. Barefoot, she balances like a circus performer, testing her weight gingerly as she

leans toward the curved wall, trying to hang a picture of waves. This is the only image in my head that hints at any desperation my mother might have felt in her long career as a military wife. If hers was a war against rootlessness and loneliness, she fought it privately, in small physical skirmishes. She made a home from whatever was given. If the kitchen in our new quarters had a window, she'd size it up as we walked through the empty rooms. The next morning, I'd wake to find she'd stitched and hung yellow curtains, creating an illusion of sunlight that tinted the linoleum and bounced off the toaster she'd polished with her sleeve.

Military stories, however mundane in topic, will engage and affect readers if they are artfully rendered and will provide us a glimpse into the human psyche. According to screenwriting guru and author Robert McKee: "A culture cannot evolve without honest, powerful storytelling. When a society repeatedly experiences glossy, hollowed-out, pseudo-stories, it degenerates. We need true satires and tragedies, dramas and comedies that shine a clean light into the dingy corners of the human psyche and society."

Compelling storytelling isn't just about events; compelling storytelling is about how those events shaped who we are today or, if we're writing fiction, how those events shaped the lives of our characters.

In any case I urge you not to wait too long before you begin your storytelling journey. During my last semester of teaching at Eckerd College in 2013, my journalism students and I began work on a documentary—our first such project—on the lives of three World War II veterans who are active members of the college's Academy of Senior Professionals. These three veterans, like most returning war veterans today, hadn't volunteered to share their stories. The academy folks, concerned about the death rate of World War II veterans—more than six hundred per day—had to coax the men into what the academy called a "cross-generational learning experience."

My students thought the task seemed simple enough: ask three gentlemen in their eighties to share a few war stories. But what happened would change us all and further prove that everyone has a story—and that every veteran bears witness to history and to the resilience of the human spirit.

Our first veteran had eagerly joined the Army and marched behind Gen. George Patton toward Germany after the Normandy invasion. He was a runner, he says. And when a commander shouted, "Runner!" above the shelling and machine-gun fire, he jumped to his feet to retrieve and deliver a message. "I remember thinking," he tells us, "you could get killed doing this." He describes young men diving into foxholes or other earthly depressions for cover; some tried hiding behind bushes and trees. Some men, boys really, went blind from a form of combat hysteria. Who knew that the mind had the power to shut off what it cannot bear to witness?

At one point during another battle, the veteran explains in the documentary, he rounded a corner and came face-to-face with a young German soldier whose weapon was pointed at him. Our veteran aimed his weapon, too, and said, half-jokingly, in a moment of total surrender, "Stick 'em up," and then depressed the wrong button on his rifle, causing the magazine of ammunition to eject onto the ground. The German soldier turned and fled. Later that day our veteran discovered that the German soldier was one of those captured and paid him a visit. The German, fearful, was certain he was to be executed, and our veteran attempted to reassure him. "Ludicrous," our veteran says on camera. "I learned that war is ludicrous." We ask him if he attributes his survival to luck or fate. "Luck," he says. "Just luck." Then he continues to describe the senseless shelling and the friends he lost—men who seconds earlier had been standing beside him. "Men everywhere were dying," he says, and dabs away a tear.

Our second veteran had joined the Navy out of college and worked on the first radar system. His father had served in the First World War, his grandfather during the Civil War. The veteran says his Navy ship was sailing with the fleet on the way to the battle for Okinawa when faced with an incoming torpedo from a Japanese ship. What the Japanese didn't know, thankfully, about the Navy's new LST (Landing Ship, Tank) was that it was flat bottomed. Our veteran describes standing watch on the deck of the LST, watching the torpedo speeding closer and closer and closer and then quietly speeding under the belly of his ship filled with sleeping sailors. If he'd been on any other ship, he says on camera, "my story would be very different . . . I wouldn't be here." He describes waves of kamikaze attacks and the discrepancy between reality and the depictions in World War II films of harsh, direct kamikaze hits. "The planes just glided in," says our veteran, using his hands to show us the eerie, ballet-like gentleness of the suicide bombers.

Our third veteran joined the British army when he was just sixteen, explaining that the British were doing so well in North Africa he was afraid the war would end before he could get there. So he lied about his age and eventually ended up in the unit depicted in the famous film *A Bridge Too Far*. The veteran becomes so emotional during portions of his interview when describing the slaughter of his men that we have to stop filming long enough for him to regain his composure. And then he is back, describing calmly his first kill of a German soldier on that bridge—a knife into the back between the ribs and jabbed up to the heart, he explains. I looked around the room at the shocked faces of my students—some in tears, others with gaping mouths.

Afterward my students—visibly emotional themselves—assisted the sobbing veteran to his car. All the way there he kept muttering, "I just wish I could have done more to save them . . . but that's war." He, like so many other war veterans since, had never shared his war stories with his wife or children for fear they would think him a murderer.

This need for repression, for containing what many veterans feel as shame, has infiltrated every generation of returning war veterans, including today's. We are just now beginning to understand, and in many cases heal, the cross-generational impact of military service.

Shortly after the 2014 release of *Red, White, and True*, I spoke to a large gathering of veterans at a book festival in Florida, urging them to write their stories—for themselves and their families. A man who looked to be in his late eighties approached me afterward and said his daughters and granddaughters had pleaded with him for years to write his military stories "before it's too late." Choking back emotion, he added, "I'm finally ready."

I nearly waited too long to discover the story about my family's military ties. During a college assignment—and I didn't return to college until my early forties—I had to record the oral history of someone who had lived during the Great Depression. I couldn't think of anyone better, or closer, to interview than my own grandmother, who was living with me in Florida at the time and who, sadly, died just three weeks after we recorded this interview.

On the tape my grandmother opens with, "Well, we were Moravians—"

I interrupt her. "What? You never told me that."

"You never asked."

True. I had grown up with the stories my grandmother had chosen to tell, and these had become woven into the fabric of what I thought I understood about my grandmother and her life as a child. Suddenly, I was on a computer, researching Moravians, marveling how this group of people had overcome religious persecution in Europe, how they had found their way to America, and how they had trekked down a dangerous wagon train trail from Pennsylvania in the 1700s, settling into what we call today Winston-Salem. For years I had banked at Wachovia, which morphed into Wells Fargo. But growing up in North Carolina and Virginia, I assumed *Wachovia* was a Native American word. Turns out, Wachovia was the name of the estate to which European Moravians fled during the Reformation. Who knew, right?

But that day, while listening to my grandmother share her life during the Great Depression, I also learned about her brother's army service during the war. Howard had been a radio operator. He left for Europe shortly after marrying his high school sweetheart, Virginia, and wouldn't see her again for years—not until Nazi Germany was defeated. My grandmother shared stories about how difficult the separation had been for Virginia, who had only a letter now and then to remind her that her husband was still alive. Virginia, like many young women, grew tired and lonely. She began to stray, and my grandmother said the family never forgave her for those transgressions, but Howard did, and they lived a long life together. What a beautiful story of forgiveness and the resilience of the human spirit.

According to my grandmother, my great-uncle didn't talk about the war. And the common courtesy back then was that you didn't ask a veteran about his service. Probably because every man of a certain age, unless mentally or physical unable, had served in some capacity, had seen his share of atrocities, and was expected to buck up and move on . . . get over it. We've learned a great deal since then about how men of that generation were truly affected. Recently, the *Wall Street Journal* published a lengthy report, "Forgotten Soldiers," in which it reveals the misanthropy surrounding World War II veterans. Veterans did not, according to the report, "put down their guns, shed their uniforms and stoically [forge] ahead into the optimistic 1950s."

During those years, according to the WSJ article, VA doctors resorted to lobotomies in an effort to relieve veterans who suffered from post-traumatic stress nightmares and flashbacks. "You couldn't help but have the feeling that the medical community was impotent at that point," Elliot Valenstein, a World War II veteran and psychiatrist who worked at the Topeka, Kansas, VA hospital in the early 1950s, told the WSJ. Valenstein claimed that doctors then "were prone to try anything."

When I first shared the premise of this book with friends and fellow writers, most assumed *On Point* would be a guide exclusively for the military veteran. *On Point* is a guide for writing the military story. As I've stated before, if you are or have been a member of a military family, you no doubt have a number of military stories you can tell. In my anthology, *Red, White, and True: Military Stories from Veterans and Families, World War II to Present*, I included true stories from spouses and grown children, and their essays are just as compelling as the essays from Iraq War veterans. If you are the parent of a military son or daughter, you, too, have several stories about how military service has affected you; at times you have probably felt pride, worry, fear, betrayal, resentment, anger, and other strong emotions.

In her poignant memoir, *Losing Tim*, Janet Burroway writes about the death of her son, a former Army ranger and government contractor. "Every suicide is a suicide bomber," she says in the opening paragraph of the book. "The intent may be absolutely other—a yearning for peace, the need to escape, even a device to spare family. Nevertheless, the shrapnel flies."

In her essay for *Red, White, and True*, "Growing a Soldier," Tonya Gutting describes the angst she felt while making a ghillie suit (camouflage clothing) for her son and of her son's certain destiny to follow his father's path. "It's one thing to send your husband to war," she writes. "You can't control him. You have confidence in his ability. You are not responsible for protecting him. It's another to offer up your son."

I recently talked with a Marine about the difficulties of separating from his family for a tour in Afghanistan. He said he managed to remain emotionless while saying good-bye to his family but fell apart when it came time to say good-bye to his dog. It tore him up that the dog couldn't understand the need for or the length of the separation. "He'll be expecting me to feed him in the morning, to throw him a ball, and I won't be doing those things for a long time." Every one of us could probably write a compelling story about the art of saying good-bye.

But no form of artistic expression happens without some degree of commitment and struggle. As writer Ben Fountain asserts, "It takes a quiet ruthlessness to carve out the time we need to get our writing done." If, as they say, life is best when we are being loved or giving love, then giving ourselves permission and time to write and reflect on our lives are two of the greatest acts of self-love I can imagine.

Writing Project

Treat yourself to a new notebook or leather-bound journal and two pocket-sized notebooks. I recommend you keep one pocket-sized notebook and ink pen in a nightstand drawer; use these for recording writing thoughts that occur to you during waking moments and, if you like, your dreams. I recommend you keep the second pocket notebook and ink pen on you at all times—maybe in the console of your vehicle, in a handbag, or in a shirt or trousers pocket.

Within your larger, primary journal, you will begin to record reflections regarding a military story that I'm going to ask you to read along with *On Point*. You'll also use your primary journal as a place for recording fragments of memories and for drafting the earliest stages of your military story.

As you stand before the rack of notebook and journal possibilities, please allow yourself to be absolutely present in the moment of selecting. Pick up several and flip through the pages. Let yourself explore which ones you are drawn to. My wish is for you to welcome a sense of reverence for this new writing life you are gifting yourself.

So, which journal feels most like the writer who resides within you? And while you're there, choose a wonderful set of comfortable gel ink pens too.

If you're someone who would prefer to document your writing journey throughout *On Point* by way of a laptop or other electronic device, that's fine too. Just be sure to back up your work regularly.

JOURNAL ENTRY 1

For your first journal entry, please choose a military title from the Recommended Military Reading section at the end of *On Point*. You'll find most of these titles in your local library. Many of them are also available in your preferred electronic reader format.

Because writing and critical reading are inextricably tied to one another, we're going to begin here with actively engaging our military reading. After you've made your selection, read the first twenty-five pages and record your answers in paragraph form to the following prompts:

> This appears to be a military story about _____ (fill in the blank with as much reasoning as possible).
> What I like most about this story so far is _____ (and explain why).

What I find most troubling about this story so far is _____ (and explain why).

What I can relate to most within this passage is _____ (and explain why, being as specific as you can—is it the setting, the timeframe, the situation, the characters' actions and motivations?).

JOURNAL ENTRY 2

After your first twenty-five pages of military reading, next record the answers to these questions in your journal:

What do you believe will be the two or three most challenging aspects of writing a military story?

What will be the two or three most rewarding aspects of writing a military story?

How, at this point, would you define success for your personal writing? Be frank. If you hope to see your writing on the *New York Times* best-seller list, then own that. If your definition of success is a memory dump on the page with a planned bonfire at the end, own that too.

Note: Once you complete Journal Entry 2, continue reading your selected military story as you read *On Point*, alternating between the two.

2

Discovering Where the Small Fires Burn

If you honor the complexity of your own life—if you grant us entry into moments that hold shame or hurt or heat, and if you're willing to follow that heat, to feel out where all the small fires burn, then your readers will trust you. —LESLIE JAMISON

As I've stated, I left the Marines with a story I never intended to share with anyone. I left after a stellar career that included two Navy Achievement Medals and Good Conduct Medals, a number of writing awards, two meritorious promotions, and a warrant officer promotion, yet I left under conditions that felt less than honorable, despite an honorable discharge. I left the Corps wracked with guilt and defeat. For many years I kept quiet about my Marine Corps service.

I was nearly forty before I finally returned to college to pursue a degree in creative writing. I still hadn't planned to share my Marine Corps stories. Besides, I wondered, who would care about my story? I was no reality TV star with a growing platform. More important, I wasn't sure my daughter was ready to know the truth about my ten years in the Marines.

As writer and military veteran Tobias Wolff states: "The very act of writing assumes, to begin with, that someone cares to hear what you have to say. It assumes that people share, that people can be reached, that people can be touched and even in some cases changed. So many of the things in our world lead us to despair. It seems to me that the final symptom of despair is silence, and that storytelling is one of the sustaining arts; it's one of the affirming arts. A writer may have certain pessimism in his outlook, but the very act of being a writer seems to me to be an optimistic act."

Not everyone can or will write and share their stories, but those of us who can and will are able to affect lives with our portrayals of what it means to be deeply human. I've never been to Vietnam, but Tim O'Brien's novel in stories, *The Things They Carried*, and Tracy Kidder's memoir *My Detachment* will forever live within me, for through their books I gained a deeper perspective about myself as a woman, a Marine, a writer, and a human being.

Nearly twenty years after my military discharge, I learned through the vehicle of a college workshop that readers, especially those without military experience, were indeed interested in my military stories, at least the short excerpts I'd crafted and shaped for workshops. Thanks to the guidance of professors and mentors, the excerpts were tied together by a narrative thread for *Eyes Right*.

But just as I was completing the first draft, a former brother-in-law blurted in front of the entire family one summer day during our annual beach vacation, "What makes you think anyone wants to read about *your* life story?" In that moment, I confess, the heat rushed to my face. But what I most need to confess is how grateful I am because his comment sent me back to work with the realization that because I was just me, Tracy Crow, a former Marine, and not a cast member of the *Real Housewives* series, I would have to write more artfully and with brutal honesty.

And so I did. The brutal honesty part, anyway. With each revision after umpteenth revision of *Eyes Right*, I delved deeper and deeper into personal reflections, examining the motivations behind every regrettable decision that had led me to sacrifice my health, marriage, and motherhood for my Marine Corps career. And what eventually led me to sacrifice my Marine Corps career to save another's career—at least that's how I saw it then.

After the 2012 release of the memoir, women serving in Iraq or those who had just returned from Iraq or Afghanistan began emailing and thanking me for telling their stories. *Their* stories? Turns out they, too, had faced extreme challenges during which they had been compelled to sacrifice their marriages with less-than-supportive spouses. Worse was hearing that they, too, were experiencing the same sort of sexual harassment, gender discrimination, and abuses of power without accountability that my generation had faced in the 1980s. I was outraged. If nothing had improved, for what had my generation and those before mine sacrificed so much? At least I could take solace in the knowledge that my story had validated so many others. That's the power of a single story.

One of the most meaningful emails, however, came from a retired male officer who said he had been stationed at Marine Corps Air Station El Toro during the 1980s. *Eyes Right*, he confessed, made him finally take ownership of his unfair treatment of women Marines during the 1980s. He thanked me for writing the book.

No one else has lived your story. Only you. Others have played roles in your life story, and you've responded to them in those roles, maybe even rebelled against them in those roles, but however you reacted, you did so for a reason. And writing your story, or retelling a story through the eyes of invented characters, provides a way for your voice to enter and elevate our overall understanding of the human experience and condition.

Should your military story be written as memoir—the truthful, artful rendering of fact—or should your story be fictionalized because of elements so deeply personal and frightening you believe they're best told through the veil of fiction? Only you can answer that question. In a later chapter I'll share with you how I prepared for the firestorm I knew was forthcoming with the release of *Eyes Right*.

But for now let's pause to clarify terms. Writing is defined—maybe categorized is the best word—by genre. Poetry, for example, is a genre of writing. So are fiction and nonfiction. The writing genre of fiction encompasses many forms: short stories, which is what we'll focus on here, though I realize you may be yearning to write a novel; novellas, short novels of about 150 pages; and of course novels. New writers often identify themselves by describing their projects as fiction novels; this is redundant because novels *are* fiction, even those based on actual events. I like how novelist Michael Crichton puts it in *Next*: "This novel is fiction, except for the parts that aren't."

Your work is fiction if you decide to take a literary license with the facts, such as inventing dilemmas and outcomes, creating composite characters, or inventing characters and dialogue. (In my memoir, *Eyes Right*, I did change several names, which is a common practice among memoirists so long as the reader is notified. You might choose to change the name of a childhood bully, for example, or an ex-spouse. While the material of your life is yours to write about, not everyone will welcome what they see as an invasion of their privacy.)

My novel, *An Unlawful Order*, released in 2011 under my pen name, Carver Greene, depicts a cover-up conspiracy surrounding a Marine helicopter with chronic mechanical failures. I based much of the novel on actual events. The helicopter crash depicted in the first chapter actually occurred five miles off the coast of Camp Lejeune, not Hawaii, as I depict in the novel. The mechanical failures I used in the novel are real-life mechanical failures of a helicopter that's now, thank goodness, been phased out of service. The majority of my characters are based on actual people associated with Marine Corps public affairs, as are many of the generals. The Middle East helicopter crashes within the novel are what some would call "ripped from the headlines." But the body of work is a novel, unlike *Eyes Right*, which is nonfiction.

Within the genre of nonfiction is a slew of subgenres, including journalism, essay writing, biography, autobiography, memoir, film and book reviewing, and travel writing. For *On Point* we'll focus on short essays and memoirs, though I suspect many of you will eventually develop these into book-length projects.

Eyes Right is a book-length memoir. Why isn't it an autobiography since I, the writer, depicted my own life? Because autobiographies tend to reveal the author's entire life story from birth until present moment. Memoir, on the other hand, reveals mostly a *slice* of one's life. In my case *Eyes Right* portrays the slice of my life that's associated primarily with my years in the Marine Corps. You've no doubt seen or read memoirs about overcoming addiction or moving beyond unthinkable loss. While each of them provided details about the writer's life before addiction and loss, the specific focus of the memoir is about the addiction or loss itself. Essays tend to explore and examine a single subject, concept, or idea; often memoirs show essayistic tendencies in places, and vice versa.

You may choose to write, for example, about only your experiences in, say, Vietnam or Desert Storm or about your six months in Afghanistan or about your Army father's return from a long deployment or about caring for your grandchildren during their mother's deployment. But the impression I want to make here is that you'll have a decision to make, for if you are going to reveal your experiences as memoir, you are entering an emotional contract with your reader that your writing is based on fact and is as close to your actual memories as is possible for you to recall. In other words, in memoir you are not inventing characters who were not really there with you in Iraq on patrol, and you are not at liberty to make up IED explosions or firefights. If during your process of writing you decide that the story is better rendered or more comfortably rendered with made-up characters and made-up events, then simply accept that you're writing fiction. Many military fiction writers assert that the easiest way for them to reach the truth about the human condition is to write without the restraints of facts and actual events. I get that. Writing my novel, *An Unlawful Order*, became an exhilarating ride on a wave of invention to which I couldn't return quickly enough each day for months. Still, nonfiction—perhaps because of my background as a journalist—more profoundly affects me as a writer and reader. Writer and writing instructor Lee Martin sums it up like this in his blog: "Fiction brings me to truths that are personally relevant, but it doesn't bring me to the same sort of truths that my work in nonfiction does."

Whatever genre you choose for expressing your military story, please remember this: the best writing reads with credibility and authenticity. The best writing takes the reader on a journey. And as long as the contract is clear from the beginning about whether the work is fiction or nonfiction, even fictitious events, if rendered with accuracy and emotional truth, will feel as real as those told through the contract of nonfiction.

In fact, memoirists sometimes struggle with making their true-life events read with credibility. But, you're probably thinking, shouldn't it be easier to write a true story? Not as easy as you might think because the memoirist is so close to the actual story and fails or forgets to clue the reader in to specific details, including the very detail the reader longs to learn most: *How were you shaped by this event?*

You're probably aware of the controversy surrounding the memoir *A Million Little Pieces* by James Frey. In it Frey writes gripping scenes related to recovery from his drug-addicted life. After Oprah Winfrey recommended Frey's book to the legions of book club followers, she discovered, along with the rest of us, that many of the events had either been fabricated or grossly exaggerated. The only time I've ever seen Oprah Winfrey angry in front of the camera was when she confronted both James Frey and his editor, Nan Talese.

Some within the writing community insist that Frey was within his creative rights, arguing that getting to the emotional truth was his goal and that if Frey felt he needed to fabricate or exaggerate events to help us, his readers, reach a deeper understanding of the emotional truth, then so be it. I disagree. Chalk up my disagreement to my years as a journalist and professor of journalism. I hold dear the contractual understanding between my work and my reader. If I'm unclear about certain details related to an event, I simply tell the reader that I'm unclear about certain details. "Here's how I remember them," I might write. Or something like, "My brother remembers our father's funeral differently, but this is how I remember it." Sometimes the details we can't remember are as telling as those we can, and it's our admission of the missing details that can also make compelling storytelling. According to Tobias Wolff in a 1998 interview for *Continuum*: "Our memories tell us who we are and they cannot be achieved through committee work, by consulting other people about what happened. That doesn't mean that at all times memories are telling us the absolute truth, but that the main source of who we are is that memory, flawed or not."

Military writer Tim O'Brien puts it this way in "How to Tell a True War Story," in *The Things They Carried*: "In any war story, but especially a true one, it's difficult to separate what happened from what seemed to happen. What seems to happen becomes its own happening and has to be told that way."

For me credibility is key. The truth tends to find its way into the world, and when it does, gone is the writer's credibility. So, why not just tell the reader what you do and don't remember? Be honest. If you can't remember, make up the rest and label it fiction.

I once drafted a short story about a troubled young man who steals dogs for the pure enjoyment of returning them to their rightful owners. The young man has lost his parents and is alone and has found that stealing and returning dogs is a way to cope with his loss. The joy of returning a pet and experiencing and sharing in that moment of union between pet and owner becomes an addiction he can't break, until one day when an owner says, "Keep the dog." The kernel of truth from real life that inspired this story is when a UPS deliveryman tossed a package against the door, the door opened, and my Cairn terrier, Molly, wandered outside. She was standing in our long driveway, possibly bewildered, when a stranger pulled over and coaxed her inside the car and took off.

We would learn all this hours later, thanks to an observant neighbor who, on hearing our panicked cries for Molly throughout the neighborhood, reported what he'd witnessed. My husband and I created an enormous sign: "Molly is missing. Please return Molly." We posted it to the gate of our driveway. We placed an ad in the newspaper and, against the advice of the well-meaning customer service representative, offered a five hundred–dollar reward.

For two days we searched and called. We posted signs throughout our neighborhood and adjacent ones. Then came the call: "I have your dog, but my granddaughter has taken a liking to her. What will you pay me to bring her back?" I tapped down the swelling anger and assured the woman we would pay the reward we had published in the newspaper. When she said she wanted more, I pleaded with her, explaining that I had the name of the breeder and that puppies from this breeder were only three hundred dollars; she'd have an extra two hundred dollars for puppy shots and the like. That's when the woman said she'd have to call back after she discussed it with her granddaughter. We didn't have caller ID back then. I didn't have a telephone number that I could forward to the police. My precious Molly was being held captive. I wasn't sure I'd ever see her again.

The woman did call back a few hours later and agreed to take the money. She said she'd return Molly after her granddaughter got out of school so that the child could say good-bye. My husband and I held our breath the rest of the day. Finally, a car turned into our drive, and a stunned Molly was handed over. Molly, the woman admitted, had been somewhat terrorized by their pit bull and cat and had eaten nothing but peanut butter for days. Molly was never the same after that trauma, and even today, some ten years later, she panics when I am out of her sight.

There you have it. From that kernel of truth I developed a short story about the troubled man who steals and returns dogs. I assigned him dark characteristics and motives, and I allowed him a lighter side as well. Revealing his dark and light sides provided a depth of character I'd like to think makes him memorable to readers.

So, will you write your story as nonfiction, or will it be fiction based on your personal kernels of truth? For now I urge you not to close the door to any genre option. Try instead to draw inspiration from military stories told through various genres. Army veteran Brooke King actually found her initial writing inspiration from Brian Turner's collection of poems in *Here, Bullet*. "It was, to say the least, eye opening for me," she stated. "Here was a soldier poet expressing his experience in Iraq. I was a bit dumbfounded that another soldier felt the same way I did about the war, that there was a way to express my anger, contempt, and confusion about what had happened to me overseas."

And that's when King began to write, even locking herself in her office for a whole day just to write. "Of course, most of it made no sense whatsoever," she said, "but the fact is that I had found a way to express the emotions I was feeling, things I could only write and didn't at the time have the guts to say out loud. I let the words on the page speak for me."

For Army veteran and best-selling writer David Abrams, a background in fiction dictated the direction of his Iraq War novel, *Fobbit*. "I feel most comfortable when I'm surrounded by hyperbolic language, invented dialogue, and fabricated details. Having said all that, however, I will say that when I began writing what would eventually become *Fobbit*, I toyed with the idea of making it a memoir. I even pitched titles to myself like *A Year in the Life of a Marshmallow Soldier* or *Soft Serve: How I Fought the War from My Desk*."

Abrams confessed he had kept a journal from day 1 of his deployment. By the end of the deployment he'd recorded scenarios and "overheard scraps of conversation" as well as reports from units on patrol. "I thought maybe I could make narrative sense of it. Ultimately, I didn't have enough to sustain a book-length narrative."

That's when Abrams discovered that by turning aside from the idea of writing a memoir—by, as he put it, "essentially turning my back on myself"—he could loosen up and create whatever he wanted on the page. "If memoir was a closet where I was confined and constricted by facts, a novel was a wide-open field where I could run and play. Once I allowed myself that liberty, once I shook off the bridle and reins, my imagination started running rampant. By inventing this hyper-real world of FOB Triumph, I could make the war more vivid and real. This involved a great deal of exaggeration, of course. I thought if I could plug my war experience into a wall outlet, if I could somehow amp up the juice on what I saw and heard and felt during my time in Baghdad, maybe I could get people to pay attention to this war."

As you continue to ponder whether you'll record your military experiences as fiction or nonfiction, consider how iconic writing instructor Janet Burroway determines her choice of writing genre: "I write fiction in order to hold a world in a pattern of imagery, memoir to witness my own past in the context of the political world, lyrics and children's books for pure delight."

Some writers and avid readers might argue that there's nothing unique about crafting a military story over, say, a story about base-ball. Both subjects, regardless of characters and setting, certainly require much the same storytelling techniques. And Abrams agrees, to a point. "You can put Kevin Powers's *The Yellow Birds* beside Ber-nard Malamud's *The Natural* and you'll find both are strong pieces of fiction about the human condition—one just happens to be about war, the other about baseball." But, he adds, "if you read a story that's immersed in military jargon and lifestyle, there's a unique aura that lends a certain authenticity to what's on the page. I'm thinking spe-cifically here of stories like Tim O'Brien's *The Things They Carried* or Phil Klay's more recent *OIF*, which is awash in acronyms and yet uses that militarese to powerful effect. [These two books] cannot be anything other than military stories set in the unique world so famil-iar to service members."

Marine veteran Thomas Vincent Nowaczyk says he makes judi-cious decisions when it comes to applying military jargon to his sto-ries. "The reader understands *bunk* inherently. The term for bed in the sea services is *rack*. Sometimes you have to forsake being a pur-ist for being a good storyteller, so you can't let your pet jargon get in the way. A reader does not normally want to learn a whole new vocabulary just to read a story."

As I've mentioned, I didn't see combat during the 1980s, and neither did a number of veterans I know who have nevertheless turned their Cold War military experiences into compelling storytell-ing. Navy veteran Jeffery Hess, who is also a successful writer and editor, says he avoided writing about his Cold War experiences for a long time because he figured "Tom Clancy's already done that . . . I can't do any better."

But during a time when Hess was working for the *Tampa Tribune* newspaper, a reporter asked why he wasn't writing about his mili-tary experience. That's when Hess began to examine and troll those memories for writing material. Since earning his graduate school degree in 2005 from Queens University of Charlotte in North Caro-lina, Hess has published a number of military essays and short sto-ries and shepherded two volumes of award-winning military fiction to publication, *Home of the Brave: Stories in Uniform* and *Home of the Brave: Somewhere in the Sand*. He is also the founder and leader of the *free* DD-214 Veterans Writing Workshop in Tampa. The group of veterans, some having participated since its inception in 2007, meets once a week to share writing and feedback. As a veteran, Hess believes in giving back to what he refers to as an underserved community and says, "The best way to learn is to teach."

My dream of becoming a writer was always simmering below the surface—it must have been—for after joining the Marines at eighteen, I became a journalist in public affairs as soon as a career move from the supply field was approved by Headquarters Marine Corps. Yet I still wasn't satisfied. Journalism involved research and reporting skills, certainly, and important writing, but I wanted to write stories longer than five hundred words shaped inside inverted pyramids with little more creativity than coverage of the who, what, where, when, how, and why. I wanted to create characters on a page so real my readers would feel as if they knew them as I had known Josephine March in *Little Women* and so many others by then. In the end I think I wanted, or needed, to tell stories that uncovered something meaningful about the human condition, something that proved we weren't all raging mad, or at least not all of the time.

While the trajectory of my journey toward becoming a writer is anything but a straight one, I can look back now and see that I'm the better writer for its indirect course. All those life experiences, which include two miscarriages, a stillborn child, three painful and failed marriages, and numerous career changes, form who I am today and how I make certain connections as a writer. Each of us comes to a writing life in our own way and in our own time. Linger over that thought for another second: each of us comes to a writing life in our own way and in our own time.

Are you ready to accept that this is *your* time and that you're on your way? Accepting your gifts and that it's your time applies to all artists, not just to writers. I'll use my mother as an example. After breast cancer and a double mastectomy in her sixties, my mother was encouraged by a friend to attend an art class because my mother no longer had the arm support for her favorite activity, gardening. During that first art class my mother discovered the artist within; after just a little prodding and instruction, she quickly produced wonderful work. In less than two years, her oil painting of tulips won the Virginia state competition, and the judge's comments declared the painting "gallery-quality work."

Bottled up inside us writers are imagination and memory, along with the uncertainty of the line between them. Writing, you're perhaps beginning to think, could be the answer and the outlet for all this stuff that constantly floods your mind throughout the day and your dreams at night.

But why *writing*?

Well, let's face it, if we were like George W. Bush discovering later in life a passion and talent for painting, we would most likely be sitting in front of an easel right now, dabbling in acrylics, or hunched over a worktable, maneuvering colors across YUPO paper in search of an image. If we were musicians, we would most likely be sitting at a piano or with a guitar, searching for the harmonic blend of notes with prose, rather than reading this book of prose.

Sure, a lucky few—though not I—are so multi-artistic that writing is merely the art du jour, and that's fine too. But most of us, I'm guessing, have always been attached to the idea of self-expression through words and have held a lofty respect for how those words form sentences and how those sentences form stories and how those stories reveal universal truths about the human condition.

Whether we're military veterans or the spouses of veterans or the grown children of veterans, our lives have been profoundly affected by military service—whether we have a firsthand knowledge of what it feels like to be hypervigilant in a combat zone or witnessed the death of a friend in a combat zone or worried that a loved one was in danger. Regardless, we have something to say. We have something to say to the world, or maybe to our families, about the military experience, and what we have to say needs to be recorded. Some would even say that those of us who can write, or who are willing to struggle with the art of writing, have an *obligation* to report and record history. We have something to say about the condition of the world and our role in it.

Today military writing has a huge, growing fan base. When I began *Eyes Right* more than ten years ago and was pursuing agents to represent the work, most of them turned me down because they couldn't image women wanting to read about another woman's military experience. That's not the case today. In fact, most of the women who have read my book aren't even prior military. What makes any book work is its ability to reach and touch others about what it means to be profoundly human, flaws and all—or as Leslie Jamison so beautifully writes, where all the small fires burn.

Writing professor and author Pinckney Benedict has been teaching creative writing for years at the undergraduate and graduate level. Benedict, who has never served in the military, nevertheless enjoys writing about the military and has even flown in the Number 7 plane of the Blue Angels, explaining: "I am not myself a particularly physically courageous or capable person, and as a consequence I'm obsessed with people who are physically brave and competent. You find a lot of that sort of person in the military. So that's the personal part of it."

The writer side of Benedict is always on the lookout for the best possible stories. "The stakes tend to be quite high in fiction with a military aspect. [In military stories] people aren't trying to pick the right living room furniture or negotiate a nourishing meal: they're trying to avoid *dying*. And those sources of tension and conflict make for an inherently powerful prose."

Eckerd College creative writing professor Jon Chopan believes that any story, military or otherwise, is an attempt to shed light on the "darkest regions of the human experience." Chopan, who also has never served in the military but writes on the subject, has said that the story of war "is at once terrible and at the same time profoundly beautiful." For him the space *between* the two extremes is fascinating and the reason he is drawn to writing about war. "It strikes me that we too often see war as existing in only those extremes, horror or a kind of beauty, born, I suppose out of the bond of men, the bond of warriors. But, because they are men, there is much more to them and subsequently much more to war, what war looks like, and what it reveals about us and our humanity."

Looking for the way into the stories of our lives often requires us to search for where the small internal fires are burning. Journaling can lead us to those places. If you're someone who tends to put journaling in the same category as the dreaded process of outlining, I urge you to rethink it. Journaling helps us control our memories before our memories control us. According to leadership trainer Robin S. Sharma: "Writing in a journal reminds you of your goals and of your learning in life. It offers a place where you can hold a deliberate, thoughtful conversation with yourself."

Don't worry. I won't force you to raise your hand and take an oath about how many times per week you journal. And I've only developed a handful of *On Point* writing projects that involve journaling. Remember that small notebook I asked you to pick up and to keep handy at all times? And the notebook you now hopefully keep at your bedside for recording the dreams that wake you in the middle of the night? My hope is that you'll become so excited about the discoveries you make about yourself and how you might one day incorporate those discoveries into your storytelling that you'll commit to journaling at least three to four times a week.

Brooke King has kept a journal since she was ten. "I loved to write when I was younger. I think that I just lost touch with it while I grew up, but found it again in Iraq. There was so much to deal with that I felt if I didn't write it down, I would explode."

King even used a journal entry in her forthcoming novel as a way to show her readers how differently everyone copes. "I believe it's important to just write it all down [at some point], even if it's illegible by the time you're done. The first step is to consciously sit down to write, the second is to just let it out on a piece of paper. I use a pen so that I can't sensor myself because I find oftentimes if I do try to manipulate my writing while I'm actively doing it, what comes out is not what I intended. I try not to sensor myself so the outcome is more organic."

Yes, even journaling about your military experience presents a few challenges. Will you, for example, feel free enough to record everything about your military experiences without fear of the metaphorical critic—or the well-meaning spouse or snooping child, your parents or another family member—looking over your shoulder? Just as with controlling the memory by writing down the details, you'll also want to control how and when your work is discovered. You should be the one who decides when you're ready to share the gritty truth about what happened in the seconds before that IED explosion or about how your squad leader fell apart during a firefight in Fallujah or about narrowly escaping (or not) a sexual assault or about receiving that knock on your door with two soldiers standing on the other side, there to offer their condolences on behalf of the U.S. Army.

About ten years ago I told a girlfriend where all my journals were hidden and that upon my death she was to rescue them from the house and give them to my daughter before anyone else found them. She promised, and because of that promise, I am able freely and honestly to write in my journals.

I'm going to plead with you a little here. Yes, I asked you to record your definition of success for your writing in Journal Entry 2, and this is where I'm going to ask you to suspend for now any attachment to a specific outcome. If this sounds a bit too Buddhist-philosophical for you, I apologize, but I have come to learn the hard way about letting go of my attachments to outcome. This doesn't mean that I can't wish for the right words as I enter into a new writing session with my laptop computer or for the right pacing within a scene of a novel manuscript or for a book that will someday matter to readers beyond my mother and daughter. Instead, I work hard on accepting that whatever comes from my writing will be a gift. Period. And this frees me to enjoy the act of creating a story on the page.

By letting go of my attachment to a possible outcome—a two-book deal with a six-figure advance, for example—I just write. I write for me. I write because of the joy I feel as I'm writing or the joy that immediately follows a writing session during which I closed out the entire outside world and did something solely, selfishly for me.

I write for me, and if the work is solid enough, the work will find its way into your hands, as it has here and now, for you are holding my words, and you and I are connected in this special way that only writing provides. I can tell you all this because of the forty-two years that passed between my decision to become a writer and the publication of my first book.

So, please be kind to yourself. Before you get caught up in outcomes, first allow yourself to enjoy the writing artist that is emerging from within. If you are just embarking on this writing journey and hope to publish your work someday, good for you. But know this: the process to publication will take several years. Even if you were to place a book today with a publishing house, the publishing process that involves manuscript revising by *you*, additional copyediting, marketing input for book cover images, and the like will take about two years before your book will appear on a shelf or among the online offerings of Amazon and others. So, please give yourself permission to detach from this outcome and concentrate more on how to record your military experiences on the page.

Writing Project
JOURNAL ENTRY 3

Now that you have your journal, set a timer for twenty to thirty minutes and write a description of your favorite childhood home or bedroom. Sure, I realize you have weightier subjects about which to write, but this beginning exercise of looking back is important. Whether you intend to write your personal military story or write a fictional military story, you and your fictional characters have a past that will need to be explored and examined for meaningful, compelling storytelling. For now, even if you're planning to write a fictional military story, please give yourself time to reflect on the person you once were while in that favorite space. Self-examination will help you later delve deeper into the minds and backgrounds of the characters you wish to create.

And if you prefer, describe your least favorite bedroom or home. Maybe you were forced to share a bedroom with a sibling, as I was for a time, or maybe even with a grandparent who snored all night. The goal here is to allow yourself the freedom to write without criticism and without concern for grammar or sentence structure. This is what writers refer to as "freewriting."

So just write what comes to mind. But be sure your journal entry is an *honest, meaningful, personal dialogue with yourself* about why this home or bedroom was, or was not, your favorite. How do you recognize a meaningful dialogue entry? Maybe this will help: if you're journaling, for example, about your dog eating a hole in the sofa while you were at work today and about the inevitable expense of a new sofa and you're not including how you feel about the dog during the cleanup and since then or about how facing another financial challenge makes you feel or about how you're awash with feelings of despair, bitterness, resentment, or helplessness, then you're not writing deeply enough. You're recording the event; you're not recording a meaningful dialogue with yourself about how you're being affected by it. A dialogue with yourself might also include a mention of other events that stirred the same feelings to the surface. Can you find similarities? If you find yourself struggling to write one sentence after another, feeling uncertain, for example, about what should be in the next sentence, try this: choose just one word from the sentence you have written and make that word the first, or one of the first words, in the next sentence. Keep doing this until you have a string of sentences, paragraphs, pages of sentences!

Let yourself go. Remember, this writing project is for your eyes only. After you complete this project, reread your passage and allow yourself a moment in which to sit with and reflect on your words, memories, and feelings. What, for example, did you leave out? Was the omission purposeful? If so, why? If not a purposeful omission, how would adding the material now affect the passage and, more important, your understanding of the memory?

3

Embracing the Writer (and Process) Within

There's no right way to tell all stories, only the right way to tell

a particular story. —TOBIAS WOLFF

I want to talk a little more about a writer's process. By this I mean the nuts and bolts of when and where to write. After completing the writing projects in chapters 1 and 2, you're most likely reaching conclusions about your personal process. You may have already discovered that you can't wait to place yourself and your journal inside a coffee shop or that you prefer the sanctity of your own home.

But the reason I want to talk about process here is to debunk certain myths people have about writers. Myths—or stereotypes, if you will—can debilitate new writers.

For starters not all writers suffer from manic depression or other psychological challenges. I know a great many writers who qualify as normal—at least the general perception of normal. Their lives are busy and purposeful. Some are full-time writers, but few of them are, because making a living from writing is extremely difficult. Bestselling novelist Stephen King states in his book *On Writing* that less than 5 percent of writers can claim to earn a living from their writing. King is certainly one of them, as are, most likely, Danielle Steele, Nicholas Sparks, and John Grisham. But I like what Janet Burroway says about money and writing in an online interview with *w3 Sidecar* after the release of her military-related memoir, *Losing Tim*: "Ambition fades. It really does. It really does become more important to do good work than to get paid or published or prizes for it. The joy really

41

does come out of the artistic struggle rather than the praise. Confidence grows at the same time [because] you care less what someone else thinks of it than what you think."

Not all writers get rich from their writing. Not all writers are heavy drinkers or on the brink of suicide. Sure, most writers have concerns about whether their writing is any good and how, if ever, it will be received. Will the work be worthy of publication? But what artist doesn't have concerns regarding how the work will be accepted?

Don't buy into the romantic Hemingwayesque image of the suffering writer. I'm so tired of this overplayed cliché (yes, that's redundant) that to be a really good writer, you must suffer and starve for your art. This isn't true. Will you have to make certain sacrifices for your writing? Certainly. And the majority of the sacrifices and challenges will be related to time. If your life is already filled with stressful job responsibilities, children, coaching Little League, or leading a Scout troop, then you'll have to sacrifice something like reruns of reality television shows, episodes of *Survivor*, or a half-hour of sleep for time spent reading good work and time spent creating your own good work.

Also, please know that not all writers write every day, though plenty of writers will insist you must. I have spells during which I write every day; these spells occur when I'm working on specific projects. But I've gone weeks, even months, without writing anything creative. I suppose the push to write every day comes from a well-meaning concern to flex the brain's writing muscle every day. I get that. I can feel the difference when I've taken a break because unforeseen life events extended much longer than I could ever have anticipated. But when I'm not writing, I'm journaling. I'm also voraciously reading. In fact, I read several novels a month.

Reading exercises the writing muscle too. I have a dear friend from my military past who so badly believed she was the next Great American Novelist but refused to read. She believed it was a waste of time to read anyone else's work. She refused to read another's work until she had become a published novelist. Besides, she claimed, "I don't have time to read because what time I have should be devoted to my own writing." Eventually, she quit writing altogether, claiming writer's block—another myth I'd like to dispute for you. If you feel blocked as a writer, open a book and read a few pages. Reach for a collection of poetry. When you engage a creative piece of writing, your writing mind awakens and ignites with creativity.

Army veteran David Abrams cited two novels that heavily influenced his approach to his critically acclaimed military novel, *Fobbit*: Joseph Heller's *Catch-22* and Norman Mailer's *The Naked and the Dead*. "No one has pinned military idiocy to the mat better than Joseph Heller," he told me. "The tangles of red tape, the complicated cogs of bureaucracy, the nonsensical rules carried out by battalions of buffoons—it's all here in the episodic story about a World War II Army Air Force crew stationed on the island of Pianosa in the Mediterranean Sea."

Like most writers, Abrams has been compiling a bucket list of books. Heller's 1961 novel had been on his list for years, "probably since the first time I heard someone use the term 'Catch-22' in a sentence and I asked what it meant." On a plane bound for Iraq, Abrams read *Catch-22* for the first time. Once in Iraq, he spent the next year "sweating out the Baghdad heat, writing Hellerish press releases, and reading brick-sized novels in my few hours of downtime." *Catch-22*, he said, read like an owner's manual for writing his own novel. "Heller could be spit-take funny in one paragraph, but chillingly sober in the next. He had a point to make and he did it not only with jokes and circular repartee but with convincing arguments for pacifism."

Abrams found structural inspiration for *Fobbit* through Mailer's *The Naked and the Dead*. "[*Fobbit*] seemed disjointed, as bouncy as a buggy ride over a potholed dirt road. For whatever reason, I picked up *The Naked and the Dead* and started reading. Apart from Mailer's usual great writing, I felt like the book as a whole was a revelation. Mailer has a large cast of characters in that World War II novel and his chapters move from one to the next like a roving camera." Abrams said he suddenly felt as if he had permission to structure his own novel "any damn way I felt—as long as it held the reader's interest and was true to the characters."

If you still hold any doubt about the effect of reading on your writing, I'll add here what Stephen King states in his book *On Writing*: "Can I be blunt on this subject? If you don't have time to read, you don't have the time (or the tools) to write. Simple as that."

To improve their game, golfers play with better golfers. The same principle probably applies to everything. A chemist studies the significant work of other notable chemists. Physicists study physicists, and so forth and so forth. Therefore, I'm baffled by those who profess they don't need to read to become proficient writers. Writing to be read requires far more than a basic understanding of one's language and linguistics, though language proficiency is also important and another perk of reading, by the way.

Noted screenwriting teacher Robert McKee says that to become a great screenwriter, we should be reading screenplays—at least one a week. That way, within a year, we'll largely know what we need to know to write a screenplay. What would happen if a writer with aspirations of publishing read a book a week? Imagine what would be learned subconsciously just by reading the work of other great writers. Chances are, through reading, that writer would mentally process all the techniques related to effective dialogue, pacing and plotting a story, and constructing interesting conflicts with stakes high enough to garner our attention from page 1 to the end.

I give myself mini-reading goals. One year, for example, I named my goal "The Pulitzer Project," with the objective to read fifty-two Pulitzer Prize–winning novels in fifty-two weeks. Whenever I came across a winner I'd already read, I either reread it or switched genres and read the nonfiction winner for that year. Halfway through the year I could already see how the reading was affecting and entering the novel manuscript I was currently revising.

The end goal, I believe, is to feed and nurture your form of artistic expression and not to punish yourself for having an artistic expression. I've known too many writers over the years who berate themselves for not writing every day and who feel like less of an artist if they're not writing every day. For a while I was one of them. During a painful time in 2007, when my third husband and I were divorcing, I was still trying to write, especially after he claimed that my writing was one of the causes of our divorce, finally admitting that he couldn't handle the fact that I was closing the door to our guest bedroom for three hours a day to write. He said he felt shut out of my life, and he resented the hell out of it. When I reminded him that for years I'd been working a "real" job such as teaching high school English and he didn't have access to me for eight or more hours a day, he said, "That's different . . . you didn't shut the door on me in our own home." I'll let you draw your own conclusions.

After he moved out, I kept trying to write. At the time I was revising a novel, but I couldn't focus for longer than a few minutes at a time. I had the entire house to myself, completely interruption free for the first time in a lifetime, and I couldn't write longer than a few minutes or a few sentences at a time. I was suffering from severe depression, not writer's block. Reality trumped the imaginary world I was attempting to create on the page each day. A close writer friend berated me for even trying. "You should be under the covers watching trash TV, not trying to write," she said. That might have worked for her, but for me it would have been too close to giving up. No way was I giving up on writing. I'd waited too long and worked too hard to build a writing life to give up on it. I'd bought into the theory that I was supposed to write every day if I wanted to call myself a writer.

And yet I couldn't write. What I could do, however, was read. Armed with two years' worth of book prizewinners, I immersed myself in the writings of others. I read and read and read. I also kept in close contact with writer friends about their projects, reading their manuscripts and providing feedback. I read writing magazines and yellow-highlighted my favorite parts. In other words, even though I wasn't physically writing, I was still engaged mentally and emotionally with my writing life and flexing that writing muscle. I was fueling up for the future.

My writing life mantra was and always has been: *Touch the business of writing every day.* Just reach out and touch it. Stay plugged in. Even a toaster that's plugged in while not in use draws a current.

Eventually, another close writer friend approached me with the idea of fictionalizing a section of *Eyes Right* into a short story for his military anthology. Working on a much shorter piece, and working with his insightful feedback and encouragement, I slowly regained my ability to work on revisions to the larger manuscript. A year later *An Unlawful Order*—a military conspiracy thriller—was published, and a few months afterward *Eyes Right* was released.

A few years later, much to my surprise, I remarried and this time to a man as passionate about his work in professional baseball as I am about writing. A few years into the marriage, we agreed that I should walk away from my college teaching position to focus full-time on my writing projects. We started the search for a new home back to my roots in North Carolina.

When my husband and I first walked through what would later become our new home, he assumed I would call dibs on the large room over the two-car garage. We climbed the stairs to the finished room, but I knew before we reached the top of the staircase that I couldn't write there. I could appreciate the roominess, the character of the vaulted ceiling, the privacy from the rest of the house, but what the room lacked, for this writer anyway, was natural light; the small windows at the top of the staircase provided a view to the back acreage but, with its southern orientation, only a tease of natural light.

"I can't write in this room," I said to my husband, who whirled around with a grin that said *I'll take it*, which meant the large bonus room would soon be filled with baseball memorabilia. My writing life would have to inhabit the light-filled but less private first-floor guest bedroom. The best feature of the room was its large eastern-facing bay window.

Some writers will tell you they can write anywhere, any time. I have dear writer friends who write best on the T in Boston or in a Starbucks. Surrounding themselves with noise and the comings and goings of all sorts of people and things seems to help them focus on what they're writing. That's pure madness to a writer like me. I've learned through trial and error that I'm the sort of writer who works best in seclusion, and with rituals. I begin every writing session, for example, with music in the background. Please don't judge me:

for some reason my music choice is the same John Mayer album, *Heavier Things*, that I've been listening to for more than ten years. After wearing out the first CD, I bought the MP3 version. I'm listening to it now, through headphones. The other day, while shopping for groceries in our local Food Lion, I felt a rushing surge to write. That's when I realized that the Food Lion was playing a song from my John Mayer playlist; I have successfully turned myself into Pavlov's dog. Writer E. L. Doctorow had his own ritual related to writing: "I sit at a desk. I face the wall. If you sit facing the wall, the only way out is through the sentences."

I have a writer friend who is grateful for the fifteen or thirty minutes of writing time she can snatch between homeschool assignments with her children. I have another friend who rises at 5:00 a.m. to squeeze in an hour of writing before she wakes her children for breakfast and school. Best-selling novelist Dennis Lehane mentioned during a workshop at Eckerd College a few years ago that he showers and dresses as if he's going to work and then enters his writing space, ready for his *job* of writing.

Why mention any of this? Because new writers always want to know about the writing processes of successful writers. New writers often ask published writers to explain their writing processes with hopes of being able to identify with a particular writer or maybe to emulate another's process. If rising early to write for Hemingway worked and he spent the afternoon fishing, then why wouldn't it work for the rest of us?

It's not that simple, I'm afraid. What works for one writer doesn't always work for another. We're mentally wired differently. And this is why I think it's important for writers to learn quickly what process of creativity works best for them. The discovery can save you time and loads of frustration.

Believe me, I've tried nearly everything. I've tried writing during a cross-country flight—surprisingly pleasant and productive, though hardly affordable—and I've tried getting up at 5:00 a.m. I've tried to write late at night and found my brain had turned to mush by then.

As I stated, our brains are not all wired the same. What works best for me may not work for you or even be possible given your lifestyle. (My writing sessions are generally from one to five in the afternoon, by the way.) Some of us have more morning cortisol than others, which is what tends to make them morning people. Others have a large squirt of afternoon cortisol, making them night owls.

When the door to my writing office is closed, my husband—during the baseball off-season, when he's actually home—knows not to disturb me unless the house is on fire. Just the sound of his footsteps on the hardwood hallway approaching my office are enough to whisk me away from my creative zone.

Years ago, when I first read Stephen King's *On Writing*, I was envious to learn that he could write in his laundry room. I pictured it dark and depressing inside that space. I'm not sure I could have produced anything under those conditions. Of course, he admits he moved up to a full-fledged writing space of his own long ago, but he's proof that, ultimately, you do what you have to do to carve out a writing space for your writing life. I'd like to think that if I were in my twenties again, I'd take the chance to write whenever and wherever I could—in a laundry room, in a closet, if necessary.

Fobbit author David Abrams was kind enough to share his writing process, and through this comic reveal proves points to which I'm sure most writers can attest:

Here's how it will go on an ideal writing day: I rise at 3:45 a.m. That's the best time for me to start the writing day. The house is quiet and it's just me and the keyboard and the cats rubbing themselves on my calves. I make a cup of coffee, add a little cream, pour a glass of ice water, and then carry them upstairs to my writing office.

It's a small room that was once my daughter's bedroom—there's still a bed in the middle of the room, but I've added bookshelves along two walls and put a few vintage typewriters (a Royal, two Underwoods) on those shelves. Along the south-facing wall there are three large windows and in front of that, I've positioned my writing desk. The street below is dark and still; the only activity comes at 6:30 when the newspaper deliveryman makes his rounds. I enter the room quietly, reverently. I set my coffee and water on the left side of the desk, and then turn on my music (classical music and movie soundtracks on iTunes shuffle). I wake up my computer, crack my knuckles, take a cleansing breath, and start typing. And I don't stop until I need to get ready to report to work by 9 a.m.

Now, that's a fantasy day. Here's the reality on most mornings: the alarm goes off at 3:45. I shut it off, roll over, and sleep another 45 minutes (quality time with my wife). Eventually, I get up, get the coffee and water, feed the cats, check the weather outside, empty the dishwasher, and then slowly make my way up the stairs to my office. Once there, I'll tell myself: "Okay, do NOT stop at Gmail, but go directly to Word and open your work-in-progress." Ignoring that voice, I browse the Internet, refresh my Twitter feed ten times, mosey on over to Facebook and laugh at the latest dumb-cat videos my wife has posted, and then check my email. Maybe I'll write that day's blog post. By that time, it's 8:30 and I'll shout with alarm, "Where did the time go?!" The time didn't go anywhere. It's always been right there, clicking at the same metronomic pace; it's me who's strayed, I'm the one who was where he shouldn't have been. I am my own worst enemy. It's amazing I ever get any creative writing done at all.

Whenever I'm teaching a creative writing class, I'm encouraging students to discover as much about their own writing processes as I'm helping them to improve their writing skills. I ask questions such as *What time of day did you work on this? Where were you when you were writing this?* By encouraging new writers to self-reflect on the patterns within their own lives, I try to help them become more efficient writers. They also become stronger, more creative, writers. Once they're alert to identifying the patterns and meaning within their own lives, they begin to assign patterns and motivations to characters in their stories.

By the end of a creative writing class, each student has a better understanding of his or her own writing process. Some will need library sanctity; others find their creative zone while immersed in the middle of a dorm common area. How do you know when you've reached a creative zone? I think the best way to describe the zone is this: you're entirely immersed in the creative process so that time and space and obligations all melt away, for you are only conscious of the act of creating. As Vietnam veteran and writer Tobias Wolff describes in the 1998 summer issue of *Continuum*: "If you're lucky, you'll experience a self-forgetfulness as you begin to write. You'll be in a larger kind of mind than is your usual habit. That's why we write. It isn't just for the product of the story or the novel, but it's actually for the experience of that bliss that you sometimes do have when you write, as you're somehow transported or elevated. It comes to you free, at first, and then you have to work for it."

Storytelling requires the writer to live in two worlds simultaneously. First, there's the world we're creating on the page. Second, there's the present world: I'm sitting at my desk this minute, mentally conscious that I'm here at my desk, trying not to be distracted by the roses outside my window or the hummingbird that continues to buzz by the window, certain that he has a purpose to fulfill with the peonies on my desk if only I'd open the dang window. But see? I'm also in the first world, for while I wrote all that, I was consciously thinking of you and of creating a visual for you so that you would feel included in my world. That's what writing is like: you're present at a desk, mildly conscious of the sudden discomfort associated with sitting too long or the bulging of a bladder, and so close to getting just the right words in the right order. When I'm writing, I enter a mysterious state of consciousness. I'm hardly conscious of my surroundings, if at all. And if my husband dares to open my office door during a writing session, he is likely to find a writer at work who suddenly transforms into a version of Linda Blair, turning her possessed head.

Part of the writing process, of course, involves how you'll write, not just where. Are you more comfortable, for example, writing by hand across long legal pads of yellow pages? A military veteran approached me in a Facebook message recently to ask how he's supposed to write if he can't type. As a former journalist in the 1980s,

I was forced by profession to trade pen for typewriter, but I assured him a great many writers still write their stories by hand and have someone type for them. Many writers are also specific about the type of paper, even the type of good-quality ink pen, they'll use. Writing isn't easy, period, but looking for excuses—such as I can't type—won't make it any easier.

Do you already have a desk that you only use during bill-paying sessions? Can you clear it for your personal writing space? Will your family support your writing time by leaving you alone, or will you choose to leave the house for a coffee shop, a park, a library, or the backseat of your car? One of my graduate school professors explained that after his day job as a technical writer in New York, he'd ride the subway home, have dinner with his family, and then leave again for a nearby coffee shop. Sometimes he'd head straight to the coffee shop for a few hours of writing before heading home to tuck his children into bed.

I can't predict what your writing process will look like or where your writing will take place, but I can promise that you will have one and that by trial and error you'll come to honor it as yours, thus speeding up the joy of your artistic writing expression.

Writing Project
JOURNAL ENTRY 4

With your new journal (and pens) in hand, visit each of these: a local coffee shop, a bookstore or library, and your favorite spot within your home. Write freely about each surrounding and how you feel within those surroundings. Are people too noisy in the coffee shop? Is the aroma of coffee too distracting? Is the library too quiet? Do you feel too pressured to buy something while inside the bookstore? How do you feel at home? Are there too many distractions—the awaiting Internet world, the favorite television show you just realized you forgot to record, the phone call or email you feel pressured to return, the dishwasher you forgot to unload, the yard that needs mowing? And as other thoughts enter your mind, such as memories from childhood about similar times, feel free to record them as well.

Under the heading "The Five Things I Admire Most about Myself" list your answers and include reasons for each. Don't hold back.

Next, record answers to this prompt: "The Five Things I Wish Most People Understood about Me."

Each answer is a door opening to a possible story, but for now just enjoy the process of writing and self-examination.

JOURNAL ENTRY 6

As previously discussed in Journal Entry 2, reading with a critical eye means thoroughly engaging with and examining a text. In our case we want to understand how writers write—in other words, how they employ certain techniques of storytelling.

Let's critically engage the military reading you've selected. After you've read fifty to seventy-five pages, record your answers to the following questions:

> The main character/hero of this story appears to be _____ (give the name and explain your reasoning) and this character's chief desire appears to be _____.
>
> The antagonist(s)/villain(s) of this story appears to be _____ (give the name and explain your reasoning), and the antagonist(s) is interfering with the main character's journey by (or because) _____.
>
> The time frame of this story takes place during _____, and I can/cannot relate to it because _____ (and explain reasoning).
>
> What I like/dislike most about this story at this point is _____ (and be sure to explain your reasoning).

Note: Continue with your reading to the end of the book, alternating between the military story and *On Point*.

Tip: Devise a life plan for your journal(s). Consider whether it's necessary to make arrangements for them in your last will and testament. You may think I'm kidding, but children of divorced parents who have remarried do not automatically have rights to your intellectual property. A spouse could decide to destroy your journals; whatever your wish, please make it known.

4

Plotting Our Stories with Timelines, Memories, Outcomes

Writing [a book or a story] is like driving a car at night. You can only see as far as your headlights, but you can make the whole trip that way.

—E. L. DOCTOROW

Recently, I received an email from a former Marine who wrote to say she'd discovered my books and wondered if I could offer any advice about how she could start writing her own military story. "I know I want to write about my experiences as a combat engineer in Afghanistan," she emailed. "I just don't know how to start."

As I discovered during the close self-examination of my own story in *Eyes Right*, I had to take an honest look back at a number of factors and pivotal moments from my childhood that contributed to my decision-making process in the Marines.

I started by drawing a line across the page. It looked something like this:

← ——————————————————————————————→

Next I marked off segments of the line to represent strong memory markers, or pivotal moments, during which the course of my life abruptly took a turn. I chose the earliest and most memorable ones. My parents' divorce, for example; my enlistment in the Marines at eighteen—most definitely a pivotal moment. My line began to look like this:

Trauma-related incidents obviously qualify as pivotal moments. Trauma-related memories create a soupy sludge of biochemical and psychological changes within our brains. Every time something triggers a memory—such as a car backfire, the smell of diesel fumes, the melody of a particular song on the radio—we get mired once again in the sludge of thinking. Our brains are on auto-repeat. While we've come to associate PTSD with military veterans, the truth is that according to the PTSD Alliance, nearly 70 percent of adults suffer some sort of traumatic event. Most PTSD-related traumas are actually related to childhood sexual assaults, rape, domestic violence, armed robberies, torture or acts of terrorism or war, and survivor's guilt. Nevertheless, a trauma-related incident most certainly should appear on your timeline as a pivotal moment.

So, let's try this. Draw a line across a page of your journal, turning the journal sideways, if necessary, for a longer line. Now identify the pivotal, or most memorable, moments. (You'll find an *On Point* Writing Project at the end of this chapter, if you'd prefer to wait. Also, even if you're planning to write a fictionalized version of your military experiences, I urge you to do this exercise; identifying pivotal moments along *your* personal timeline and reflecting on them will guide you toward creating interesting pivotal moments for your fictional characters.)

After determining my pivotal moments, I chose one, just one, and began writing everything I could remember about that particular time in my life. For *Eyes Right* the first memory I ever recorded was learning to fire on the rifle range so that I could accompany Col. John I. Hopkins's Fifth Marine Regiment to Twentynine Palms, California, for newspaper coverage of the regiment's combined arms exercise. In 1981 no woman had ever been allowed to accompany Fifth Marines on a combat exercise, and the fact that I had never even qualified with a rifle was a huge sticking point with Hopkins. So, he issued a challenge, one he never believed I'd overcome, given how only women in military police or recruits in boot camp were allowed on a rifle range.

Eventually, I found a way, and the resulting story of my experience extolls the details of what women like me had to go through in the 1980s to prove we could do our jobs. I was also a wife and a new mother and had to overcome the emotional challenges attached to leaving behind my domestic life. My first husband, also a Marine, was not always the most supportive and couldn't help himself, it seemed, from using our infant daughter as a weapon of guilt. And what a weapon. Instead of encouraging me toward career challenges, he did all he could to thwart them. In hindsight he was no worse at this than any man of his generation during that era. But I wanted more, and the struggle for more accomplishments than being a wife and mother obviously, sadly, led to the downfall of our marriage. All this is included in that one short memoir, which was triggered by recording the rifle range memory on my timeline.

After writing about my experiences on the rifle range and about being the only woman in the middle of a desert with hundreds of other Marines, I chose to write about an earlier pivotal moment on my timeline. In this one I'm newly married when my husband and I receive orders to Okinawa, Japan.

We landed November 4, 1979, unaware that while we were crossing the international date line, Iranian militants had stormed the American embassy and taken hostages. I had forgotten this detail about our Okinawa arrival until I was freewriting everything I could remember about that year in Okinawa. You see, I had intended to write about my first impressions of life in a foreign country as a naive twenty-year-old who had hardly been outside of North Carolina. But I knew that to accurately capture my story about my experience in Okinawa from 1979 to 1980, I would also have to reveal the most dramatic events of that year: my surprising pregnancy of twins and the subsequent stillborn death of one of my little girls.

For this pivotal moment I began freewriting about everything I could remember about arriving in Okinawa: the long flight; my swollen feet; all the strange billboard symbols in Japanese; the relief at seeing familiar symbols such as Coca-Cola and KFC; the laundry that shimmied on clotheslines of high rises in downtown Naha; the first ride in a car on the left side of the road; the strange, potent smells; the sights and sounds of the island; my husband's friend who showed up to transport us to base and his discussion about the Japanese Yakuza and how they severed the tips of their pinkie fingers as signs of loyalty.

After a number of revisions that included feedback from a creative writing professor and fellow writing students, I crafted a paragraph of those earliest memories:

Naha is the busy capital city of Okinawa Prefecture, on Okinawa Island. Taxi drivers were blaring horns. Okinawan children in navy and white school uniforms circled magazine stands and bus stops. An old woman with bright eyes and no teeth, wearing a knee-length gray tunic and slip-ons, smiled at me as she walked by, swinging a full plastic grocery bag that balanced her bowlegged sway. I was surrounded by a sea of colorful billboards, marked with strange symbols and Asian faces. Most advertisements were impossible to make out. Others were easier: a Coca-Cola billboard across the street; the face of a young, Asian woman, delicate, lotus-like, smiling beside the Nikon camera she held in her palm.

Here's the third paragraph of that memoir I eventually titled "Kyoko's Mirror," which, after many revisions, appeared in a literary magazine before its inclusion in *Eyes Right*:

My feet, swollen from the nineteen-hour flight, were spilling out of my high heels; each step felt as though I were walking on the tops of my ankles. At least my feet were managing to move forward. My mind was still refusing to budge across the International Dateline. I hadn't wanted orders to Okinawa. A month earlier, I had been four months pregnant in Jacksonville, North Carolina, planning our baby's nursery. One evening, Tom came home crestfallen by the news that he was being shipped overseas for a year. We knew military orders separated couples all the time: but for some reason, we had expected our first year of marriage to grant us immunity from such things as military separations and miscarriages.

By the time I began writing about this experience in Okinawa, nearly twenty years had passed. Yet I was stunned by how many details came flooding back once I identified the Okinawa year as a pivotal moment on my timeline and unlocked that mental compartment. But details are just that, details. What our readers want to learn more than anything is what writer William Faulkner described as "the human heart in conflict with itself."

Here's a paragraph within my memoir that reveals the narrator's psyche—I'm the narrator, of course:

> Tom and the lieutenant shared stories about the Marines they had lost touch with through the years. In the backseat I held firmly onto the armrest of the car door with my right hand and with the left, balanced my weight against the back seat as we whipped around curves, passing fields and fields of sugar cane, the sudden spring-up of villages, and Mama-sans who were toting groceries in their arms and babies on their backs. I thought again about the baby Tom and I had lost, the loss we had both mourned: yet hadn't I detected Tom's relief? Neither of us had wanted a year's separation. The Yakuza severed pinkies to prove loyalty. My body had given up a child.

Can you see why I included this first day in Okinawa as a pivotal moment on my timeline? And how freewriting about that first day provided a pathway toward a story? No doubt, you have a number of first-day experiences that are just as memorable and pivotal. Each has the potential to open a door to a story within your life and, quite possibly, toward self-reflective connections you might not have considered. Be sure to record them on your timeline. Choose one and begin freewriting. Remember to include the self-reflections in your freewriting. What counts as a reflection? Anything that refers to how you felt or reacted within a pivotal moment. If you can, and are willing to, answer this question: *How did it make me feel?* Your answer may lead you to other pivotal moments during which you had a similar feeling or reaction—a beginning toward identifying meaningful patterns. Even fiction writers must be able to reveal why their characters react to circumstances as they do, which is why developing a fictional timeline for characters is such a helpful tool.

If you've been journaling throughout your life, or at least throughout your military experience, I envy you. Your task of triggering memories and pivotal moments should be an easy one. Gather your journals and begin rereading with a handful of color highlighters. Consider highlighting specific events in one color—use a different color to highlight anything that resembles a self-reflection.

If, like me, you didn't keep journals about your military experiences, don't despair. Instead, record on your timeline the pivotal moments that readily come to mind. When you begin to freewrite about a single pivotal moment, memories of others are likely to appear. Take a moment to record the new pivotal moments on your timeline and use your journal as a way of recording details and self-reflection that you'll eventually incorporate within your storytelling.

Remember, even if you decide to write fiction, reading about your own reflections from the sense of *Looking back, what I know now* will help you build depth for your future fictional characters. What, for example, was the dominant feeling during a pivotal moment of your life that made it so memorable? Was it fear, shame, humiliation, happiness, worthiness, vindication, or empowerment? Those experiences and feelings can be assigned to your fictional characters. Try exploring this possibility in your writing: *Why did I*, the narrator of my own life story (or why would my fictional protagonist), *feel as I did during that pivotal moment? What about the life that came before that pivotal moment caused me* (or my fictional protagonist) *to feel such emotions as fear, shame, humiliation, happiness, worthiness, vindication, or empowerment?* Your readers will want to know. Dare I say—*you* will want to know. Look at it this way: writing that offers little or no reward for you, the writer, will offer little or no reward for your reader.

Besides creating a timeline to uncover story opportunities, consider a look back at old photographs or home movies. Amber Jensen, the wife of an Iraq War veteran, found inspiration from photographs for her memoir "Memory Sky," published in *Red, White, and True*. Here's an excerpt revealing how Jensen incorporated the photographs as a reference point:

> Grandpa Dayton had always been a source of questions for me. I knew him from black and white photos and fragments of stories sprinkled here and there at holiday meals and afternoon coffee like powdered sugar over brownies; Blake knew Grandpa Dayton only from my versions of those stories. And yet Blake understood Dayton in ways I could not.
>
> Once, noticing a small black and white photo tucked in a china closet, Blake said: "Dayton was a first sergeant? You never told me that." I'd never told him because I hadn't known. "The patch on his uniform," Blake explained. "First sergeant. That really meant something, especially in those days." I had studied that photo for years, hoping to gain some understanding of the mysterious man who died so young, so long before I was born. I had memorized the slope of Grandpa Dayton's nose, the droop of his eyes, and his faint smile lines. But in a glance, Blake had made meaning from the photo, and established a connection. To Blake it was a simple, objective interpretation.

Fiction writers might also incorporate the device of photographs as a way of developing a past for their characters. A character, for example—let's say he's a young man—might happen upon a shoebox of photographs while clearing out his mother's attic after her death. Among the photos are several of a man in a military uniform that could be World War II era—but someone our character doesn't recognize. On the back of each photograph, however, is a message in his mother's handwriting. The messages are brief but filled with tenderness. (I'll let you, the fiction writer, determine the messages, but take my word for it, the tone is tender.) The man's name is never included, and neither are the date and location. Who is this mystery military man? Our character wants to know, is yearning to know. His search for answers will, of course, lead him to a truth his mother never intended him to discover, or did she? After all, why did she hold onto and leave behind that shoebox of photos? Did she really just forget? Did she become too frail to climb the staircase to the attic? You're the fiction writer; you get to decide.

So, images are powerful. Images have the ability to catapult us back in time or propel us to embark on a search for missing pieces. Just when we think we've forgotten the quality of his gravelly voice, her vanilla scent, the unrelenting rain that one particular summer afternoon, a photograph conjures it all. Isn't this partly the reason we love taking photographs? We're preserving a moment because even the happiest memories tend to fade too quickly. The drama in our lives, and our tendencies to remember and relive that drama and the fear or shame or dread associated with it, gets buried deeply into the dendrites of our brains. The less traumatic events, such as most of the Latin we learned in high school, is eventually pruned by the brain. Where does it go? I don't know. It just . . . disappears. Or it fades to such an extent that we might even question whether the event actually happened. Was it raining that afternoon or not? Who won last year's Super Bowl? All I remember is the party—my friend's amazing seven-layer Mexican dip and how annoyed I was that people kept talking during the commercials, my favorite part.

You might also find your path into a story and another pivotal moment by looking over family letters. Perhaps you're fortunate enough to have a parent or grandparent who, while he couldn't or wouldn't talk much about his military service, left clues behind in the letters he sent home. Even in the absences between sentences, you might find creative ways to relate, reflect, and compare another family member's military service with your own. If you are writing about your own life, you become a reporter, in a sense, who is curious to know all that's possible to know about the life that led up to the beginning of, well, you.

I love Beverly Jackson's story. Jackson never knew her father. He was a tail gunner on a B-17 during World War II when his plane was shot down over France. Her mother would eventually remarry, and her stepfather didn't welcome talk about Jackson's father. Many years later—in fact not until after her mother's death—Jackson began an intense search to learn more about her biological father. Thanks to the Internet and the encouragement of friends, she flew to a small village in France. The villagers provided a hero's welcome. They took her to see the "Wing Shed," which is made in part from the wing of her father's plane. Here's an excerpt of Jackson's story:

> We have parked the cars off an isolated farm road, to visit the Wing Shed. It is an old-fashioned lean-to, long abandoned, really just two walls on some poles stuck in the soil. Its weathered walls are pale gray metal, constructed from their prize, the wing of the *Big Bitch*. After decades of hard winters, the metal structure cants perilously, sinking in tall weeds. A somber little group of nine, we congregate on a muddy cow path alongside an irrigation ditch.
>
> Huddled under umbrellas in the spring rain of Brittany, we have to cross an irrigation ravine to get to the shed, which, after sixty-five years, is bonded to its surroundings. Grass sprouts from the crevasses of its seams. Under this flat gray sky, I feel like a melancholy child in my old body—a woman close to seventy. A father could not recognize his child in this gauzy light.

Is your mind reeling now from all the story possibilities? Are the pivotal moments within your life story springing to the forefront of memory? If you're writing fiction, are you forming a clearer understanding about the past for your protagonist?

If you're ready, fling open the doors to your pivotal moments and find the stories within. Remember to monitor your feelings and to seek counsel from your health professional, trusted friends, or loved ones if you need to.

Writing Project

In your journal, turning it sideways if necessary, draw a straight line across the middle of the page. This will become your life's timeline. Use several pages or several lines if you must. Pinpoint the most memorable events of your life. A first pet? A first kiss? Not making the college football team in senior year? Taking the oath to join a branch of the military? Be open to recording positive and negative memories—any memories of moments in your life during which you can look back now and realize the course of your life changed because of that moment.

JOURNAL ENTRY 8

Now choose one of the moments, either from childhood or from your military life. Set a timer for twenty to thirty minutes and freewrite. Don't worry about using perfect grammar or syntax. Just write. Write what you remember. Write what you don't remember. All details, including those you don't remember, can become quite revealing. Allow yourself this gift of freewriting time, and any fears you may be harboring about facing what writers refer to as the "blank page" are likely to dissipate soon.

Now that you have a pivotal moment of your life captured on the page through freewriting, record the conclusions you can make today about the person you were during that moment of your life. Were you, for example, mad at the world? Why? Were you mad at your parents or a boyfriend or girlfriend or sibling? At your military superiors? Your spouse? Why? What didn't they understand about you?

Looking back, what didn't you understand about those with whom you were at odds? What do you wish you understood then about the situation that you know now?

Finally, regarding that pivotal moment . . . it had an outcome, right? Was it a positive outcome? A negative one? Record those details here. Whatever the outcome, are you now harboring regrets? And looking back, what were the driving *motives* behind your decisions surrounding that pivotal moment? Consider answering this prompt: *Knowing what I know now, might the outcome have been different, or must I accept that the outcome most likely would have been the same? If it would have been the same, why?* Remember, even if your goal is to write military fiction, a deeper understanding of motive will help you shape compelling characters on the page. Your readers will want to understand, root for, and empathize with your characters; they won't feel much for thinly portrayed characters.

JOURNAL ENTRY 9

Now look *forward* along your timeline. Can you find another dramatic moment that connects on a thematic or emotional level with one from your childhood? Is there a time in your military career, for example, when you felt or reacted the same way as you did about that childhood event? I'll share a personal example: I'm terrified of going underwater. If there's such a thing as reincarnation, I've drowned in every former life, and I nearly drowned when I was a child. Today I won't even get my face wet in the shower. So, when I had to jump off of a diving board in boot camp, I was gripped by tremendous fear. In the writing of an essay, I found a way to tie together both events. So, what similarities can you find between two incidents from your life? What differences? It's even possible that what you'll write about is how differently you reacted during a military experience because of what you had learned about yourself, others, and life in general from that childhood dramatic event.

Are you beginning to see how writers tie events together? Start writing!

JOURNAL ENTRY 10

Now take that same pivotal event and freewrite it as fiction, entirely changing the outcome. Afterward think about which one was easier to write. Which version is actually closer to the emotional truth and why?

Locate photographs of your military experience or photographs of a family member's experience. Choose one or two photographs that stir something emotional within you: joy or melancholy or another emotional state. Even better if you can find one photograph that elicits a joyful memory and another one that causes you great reflection of a less joyful time.

Now, choose one of the photographs to freewrite about in your journal, including everything you can remember about the story leading up to and just after the moment the photograph was taken. Who took the photograph? Is it a selfie? What do you remember about the setting? About the people with you, if they're also in the photographs? Since we generally take a photograph to have a visual record of an event, what is the significance behind the event? What happened in the moments leading up to and just after the photograph was taken?

After freewriting about the emotions and circumstances behind the first photograph, move toward the second one and do the same thing.

And finally, how can you link the two photographs and the two moments together? What if you were to look at the first photograph, for example, while pondering a prompt such as: *What I couldn't know then is . . .* or *When I said good-bye that day . . .* ? Refer to the emotions and circumstances in the second photo, or vice versa.

Another way to get started in your writing is to spend a little time on research. Notice, I said a *little* time. Too often writers get so caught up in the act of research that it becomes an excuse not to write.

But let's say you want to write about your time overseas or spent on a particular base or ship. Take a few minutes and do a Google search. Sure, I realize you were there, but there are still things you won't remember or maybe don't know about the country, and these facts might prove useful. When I was writing the section of my memoir about my time in Okinawa, for example, I had to do research to ensure I was remembering what side of the island my apartment faced. Was our apartment actually facing the South China Sea, as I remembered it, or the Pacific? And when I wrote the Carver Greene novel with its setting in Hawaii, I actually flew to Hawaii for two weeks while I worked on the revisions of the first draft to ensure I would be accurate, and yet I still had to use the Internet to clarify many of the details. Oftentimes, just spending a few minutes researching where you've been will open a tiny window into memory and set you off on a writing spurt.

Record facts about a place that is mentioned in your Journal Entry 11 freewriting exercise related to photographs.

Record how these facts now help to shape the story related to the photographs.

5

Developing Characters, Conflicts, and Connections

Figure out what it is that makes your heart beat hard, what keeps you awake at night, what you don't want to face, what shames you, what haunts you. That's your source of power. That's your [storytelling] material.

—KYLE MINOR

You've been reading all your life, so you innately understand that a great number of stories develop from an architecture of beginnings, middles, and ends. Quite possibly in your *On Point* freewriting exercises, you've been creating this very architecture without thinking about structure. (While I realize this particular story design is but one of many, it is also the most familiar and basic, which is why I've chosen it as a model for the stories you're developing at this phase of your writer experience. Your growth as a writer will eventually lead you to other frameworks.)

In the beginning characters and conflicts are introduced; just as with the building of a home, for example, a foundation is poured. As the story proceeds, the stakes for the characters are raised, and tension is ratcheted up. New conflicts or dilemmas—those with the greatest intensity that might include a crisis or a reversal of action—develop within the middle of a story, also known as the climax, and compel characters to make tough, often gut-wrenching, decisions. The ending includes the falling off of action—the resolution as a result of the actions taken by characters during the climax. Nineteenth-century

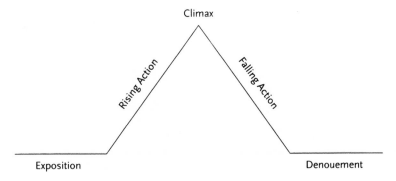

Climax

Rising Action

Falling Action

Exposition

Denouement

Fig. 1. Freytag's Triangle.

playwright and novelist Gustav Freytag illustrated this story structure in what has become known as "Freytag's Triangle."

In his famous "Eight Basics of Creative Writing" Kurt Vonnegut, author of the military novel *Slaughterhouse-Five*, states: "Be a sadist. No matter how sweet and innocent your leading characters, make awful things happen to them—in order that the reader may see what they are made of."

Aristotle believed that plot, the arrangement of direct or indirect challenges to the goals of a protagonist (or narrator in a memoir), is the single most important aspect of storytelling. This arrangement of incidents keeps our reader hooked and asking, *And then what happened?*

At the heart of plot—at the very heart of compelling storytelling—is conflict, both internal and external. In the *On Point* writing projects leading up to this chapter, I've been leading you toward writing about internal and external conflicts.

Without conflict, which is present even in the most humorous of stories, we have no interesting story. Without conflict we have a simple anecdotal rendering of an experience, not a thought-provoking, compelling story with stakes—such as those related to birth, death, sex, money, friendship, family, identity, and spirituality—that continue to rise for characters and illuminate the often gut-wrenching choices that reflect what it means to be human, causing us to ponder what choices we would make under the same circumstances.

In his book *On Becoming a Novelist* John Gardner writes: "In the final analysis, real suspense comes with moral dilemma and the courage to make and act upon choices. False suspense comes from the accidental and meaningless occurrence of one damned thing after another. The wiser or more experienced writer gives the reader the information he needs to understand the story moment by moment." Involving the reader this way, according to Gardner, will compel the reader to feel genuine concern for the characters.

When I was reading over submissions for *Red, White, and True*, I discovered that most new writers were sending me little more than anecdotes or, even worse, their official military biographies that contained nothing more than a rambling list of their duty stations, years at each, job titles, and ribbons and medals. All this information is important to leave behind for our families, of course, but without the storytelling aspect of conflict, this information falls flat for readers outside our family. Writer and professor Pinckney Benedict explains that military writing has special challenges: "Probably the toughest is communicating a highly specific, closed culture—like a religion, in many ways—to folks outside that culture to whom it may be quite alien."

This doesn't mean that you should avoid incorporating military terminology into your writing. Quite the opposite. In fact, a graduate school professor encouraged me to incorporate more military terminology in my final thesis of *Eyes Right* so that the reader would get a greater sense of its authenticity. But Benedict is right in that the writer has to juggle what the reader will be able to intuit, without pausing to look up unfamiliar words, with the value of using terms that are specific to military life. If we break the reading spell too often, then they will lose confidence in us as writers. Readers can tell from page 1, from the way the words are arranged on the page and punctuated, whether or not they're in the hands of a capable storyteller.

In an anecdote or biography the missing element is suspense, which is a by-product of conflict. A writer creates suspense by building anticipation. Will the protagonist succeed in attaining a goal or fulfilling a yearning? Without conflict and a buildup of tension—that friction between two opposing forces—we aren't much invested in the outcome of the reading. Every reader wants at least one character that he or she can root for, according to writer Kurt Vonnegut in "Eight Basics of Creative Writing."

We might read a funny anecdote about someone's military service and think, "That's nice" or "Yep, I can relate to that." But anecdotes are rarely memorable unless they are ours or belong to someone close to us. The reading of anecdotes isn't particularly memorable. And the reading of a military bio of duty stations and job listings is even less memorable. Sure we may be impressed to learn that a loved one earned not one but two Purple Hearts or when and how he earned that Medal of Honor. But what we're really hungry for is the story that accompanies each of those medal-earning experiences. Readers want to know how these experiences shaped who we are today or, if we're writing fiction, how our main character—referred to by writers as the protagonist—has changed. In other words, readers want to be emotionally invested.

When I began writing about my experiences in the military, one of the greatest challenges I had to overcome was the guilt I felt in revealing even the tiniest of negative details about the Marine Corps. After all, I had been a trained public affairs reporter and later the officer in charge of public affairs for the New River Air Station in Jacksonville, North Carolina. My job for nearly ten years had been to tell the Marine Corps story in ways that enhanced retention and recruiting. My job had been to spin and polish every incident so that it appeared all was fine in the Corps and that all Marines were trained for the fight against the Evil Empire. When, as a sergeant on assignment to cover a desert combined arms exercise with the Fifth Marines in 1980, I described the negative effects of heat on the Marines, an officer vigorously crossed out those sentences. There's a reason Harry Truman claimed the Marines had a propaganda machine nearly as good as Stalin's.

But in understanding the craft of storytelling, I learned that there are no angels or demons. The goal of a serious writer is to create a story or to reveal an essay of one's life that is as richly layered as life itself. How do we know light without experiencing the dark? How do we know good when we encounter it unless we've also encountered evil? In my memoir I wrote as fairly as I could about the antagonistic aspects of my life as a woman Marine. In my military novel, *An Unlawful Order*, I conveyed a story loosely based on actual events about a mechanically flawed helicopter that's no longer in operation, thank goodness. But before the Corps would stop flying this bird, dozens and dozens of Marines lost their lives in crashes too conveniently blamed on weather elements. I didn't write the book with any sort of revenge in mind; revenge can be a dangerous, risky motivator. Instead, I used the premise of the flawed helicopter and the horrific crashes to reveal the motives for why my characters insisted on keeping this bird in the air.

During the writing process of both my memoir and novel, I wrestled with guilt. How could I turn my back on the Corps and write even the smallest of negative details? Later I would come to think of this writing as honest, even brave. Had I glorified the actions of my characters during the war scenes within the novel, I would not have revealed an honest portrayal of the human experience.

As you contemplate your own stories, I urge you to consider your personal motives for each of them. Even a spouse who became an ex made us happy at one time and had qualities we admired, or else why did we marry? Be sure to consider the multilayered complexities of a whole life, not just the actions of a single day. For me this is the most exciting aspect of writing: self-discovery, even when I'm writing fiction.

For years as a new professor, I taught English composition and rhetoric. Each semester I began with Aristotle's theory regarding the must-haves of persuasive writing. Even though I was primarily a creative writing instructor, I found his theory provocative for my own creative work. According to Aristotle, truly persuasive writing, for example, must seek to appeal to its audience on three levels: on an emotional level (pathos), an intellectual level (logos), and a credibility level (ethos). As I worked on *Eyes Right*, I searched for ways to ensure I was including all three. To satisfy the emotional level, I wrote my way toward the darker side of experiences, exposing my intentions and motivations behind good and bad decisions. To satisfy the logical side, I examined my actions from the safety of hindsight and double-checked my facts. To help foster an air of credibility, I included what I felt were just enough military terms and cultural references to keep my readers grounded in time and place; too many military terms might have alienated most readers without military backgrounds.

You would think that writing the military story would easily include conflict, and it should, but often new writers get too caught up in the events of the moment to fully identify the wants and needs of a protagonist—who is you, if you're writing memoir, and your created characters, if you're writing fiction—and how those wants and needs are being thwarted by antagonistic forces. Every character, including you if you're writing memoir, should want *something*, even if, as Vonnegut states in his rules for creative writers, "it is only a glass of water."

Writers identify conflict in storytelling on four basic levels: person versus him- or herself; person versus person; person versus nature; and person versus society or ideas.

Let's take a closer look at each level of conflict.

1. *Person versus him- or herself.* How many times have we heard that someone is his or her own worst enemy? We often get in our own way of sound judgment, don't we? And this level of conflict makes for compelling storytelling. Hard as it was in *Eyes Right*, I had to go to those dark places and admit the truth about myself and the motivating factors behind bad decisions. What I hadn't expected, however, was the outpouring of support from my readers for revealing the internal conflicts I had wrestled with throughout my nearly ten years as a Marine while also being a wife and a mother. During my twenties I needed to prove, for reasons revealed in the book, that I was the right Marine for the job, even though I was a woman during a time when women were rarely looked at as anything but a distraction to good military order and discipline.

Brooke King notes about her own military writing: "I can say with honesty that if I hadn't explored my inner self, I would never have been able to reflect it in my war writing," adding: "War isn't so much what happens, but how people deal with it during and afterward. The most important thing about writing a military story is to make it come from the heart, to tell YOUR story your way. Don't be afraid to tell that story. Be confident in your ability to show the world through your eyes what it was like to live through such a tumultuous time."

The conflict level of person versus him- or herself applies to fiction as well. David Abrams's best-selling novel, *Fobbit*, provides many examples of internal conflict, including this one:

And yet Abe himself did feel shame over what had happened at Intersection Quillpen. He'd been too slow to react, too hesitant to commit to the bullet. Why was that?

He didn't know and he'd been kicking himself from here to Sunday ever since, agonizing over the indecision. Had it been an urge to protect the soldiers inside that Abrams tank and the gathering Iraqi onlookers? Was it a question of wringing his hands for one minute too long as the moment of opportunity peaked and other factors came into the picture to clutter the situation? Or maybe he was just afraid of picking the wrong door in this "Let's Make an Iraqi Deal." He was pretty sure his grandfather never had one stuttering moment of waffle-waffle before sticking his bayonet in a Jap's throat.

The last line about Abe's grandfather provides a hint about why Abe is experiencing such jarring internal conflict and gives us a glimpse at its depth and fuller meaning.

In "How the Military Turned My Father a Genius," an essay that appears in *Red, White, and True*, Kim Wright reveals a more humorous take on the person versus himself conflict. Her father, a World War II sailor, has just taken a shipboard IQ test, with hopes of qualifying to work on the new technology, radar. The scene opens with his commander's observations regarding the IQ test results:

"Son, did you know you're almost a genius?"

Note the word "almost." The Air Force defined a genius as anyone with a 140 IQ and my dad's tested at 138. But this was enough to get him into the radar program.

No one was more surprised by this news than my father himself. Nothing in his life up to this point had indicated there was anything unusual about his level of intelligence. But he suddenly found himself in a training program predominantly populated by, as he put it, "a bunch of those ROTC-type boys." During the next eighteen months, they studied, they trained, they served as air traffic controllers, they gambled, they drank, they had low level heat strokes in the desert, and on their days of leave, they ventured into Tangiers for the sort of adventures men don't discuss with their daughters. And my father got a new vision for his future. He began to see himself as someone who could hang with educated and advantaged people and keep up just fine.

A sweet little story, right? Pottery town boy makes good, grabs a chance at a new life. But here comes the twist. One day my dad is in the control room monitoring the position of several planes. There was a larger than usual number in the sky over the base and he was a little anxious, so he made a mistake. He touched the screen with the metal fountain pen he was holding in his hand. He was also sitting on a metal chair and immediately a bolt of electricity ran through him, knocking him unconscious and sending the chair flying across the room where it crashed into a wall.

When he came to, his first thought was that he was no longer smart. He had probably suspected all along, to be honest, that the first IQ test was some sort of fluke, perhaps incorrectly graded by a man too seasick to see straight. He was so worried that the bolt had zapped him back to ordinary that they gave him a second IQ test.

It went up two points. He was now officially a genius.

2. *Person versus person:* This category of conflict features the classic struggle of protagonist versus antagonist. If you are writing memoir, you are the protagonist of your own life story. This doesn't mean,

however, that you get to be the only hero of your life story, for your reader will find that portrayal too self-aggrandizing. But in your life story, in everyone's life story, are people who issue challenges or create seemingly unfair obstacles for us. I write about several of these people in *Eyes Right*. One was the regimental commander who said in 1981 that if I wanted to be his beat reporter, I had to first qualify with the m-16 on the rifle range. A few problems there: only women military police officers were allowed on the rifle range, and I had only two weeks to make all this happen. So, this becomes a story about overcoming a colonel's sexist viewpoints. Also, I had to overcome my husband's arguments that included comments such as, "Why can't you just be satisfied with being the wife of a military officer and a mother to our daughter?" Do you see and hear the conflicts—both person versus person and the hint ("why can't you be satisfied . . . ?") of person versus herself?

In his memoir, *It Happened on the Way to War: A Marine's Path to Peace*, Ryan Barcott reveals the potential person versus person conflict through his father's response to Barcott's ROTC scholarship: "His lukewarm reaction bothered me until I realized that it came back to the Vietnam War, a war that he believed was so misguided by generals and politicians that it was criminal. His combat experience made him eternally skeptical of any institution's ability to protect the best interests of individuals, and he was especially conflicted about the Marine Corps."

In a short memoir piece for *Red, White, and True*, former Marine Thomas Vincent Nowaczyk reveals the physical and emotional abuse he and his Parris Island platoon suffered at the hands of their drill instructors, who were later court-martialed and imprisoned. Here is one section that provides a glimpse of person versus person conflict:

I have tried to forget how it felt to watch Private Fuckwad (the drill instructor's pet name for one of our recruits) finally piss his own pants, and the look of humiliation on his face when he did, and the way he tried to hold back the tears as piss ran down his shiny black boot into a puddle on the deck. I have tried to forget the shock of Sergeant Smith screaming about the piss. I cannot forget the revulsion, disgust, and utter self-loathing I felt when Sergeant Smith made Private Fuckwad roll around in his own piss to mop it up.

I can't forget the full length of Sergeant Smith's fist and forearm through my gut and damn near out my back. Or of tripping backward over my footlocker when he slammed my head against the steel post of my rack, and slammed me again, head first, onto the cement deck.

Here's another example of person versus person conflict from the opening of Zoey Byrd's short story, "Flying the Hump," in *Home of the Brave: Stories in Uniform*:

It was a good lesson on how not to fly a plane.

The c-47 Gooney Bird was overloaded, but Major Nettles told the crew chief, "Never mind. If we crash it's your fault."

Truth be told, the Major wanted to set a record for tonnage moved in a day. He had a flair for the unusual, wanting his crew to make the newsreels back home. Sergeant Huff saw that the crew chief had overloaded the plane and said nothing. Huff had flown with the Major once before and knew him to be taciturn and unapproachable on the ground, but a daredevil in the air.

Whether you choose to write your military stories as fiction or nonfiction, your goal will be to reveal a protagonist and antagonist with equally compelling conflicts. In Byrd's example she has set us up early with enough expectation to engage our interest. We don't yet know for certain the plane will crash or whether Huff or the crew chief will eventually stand up to the reckless major, so we are compelled to read on.

One way to create compelling fictional characters is to draw from personal experience. The fictional characters in my Carver Greene novel, *An Unlawful Order*, are all based on actual Marines I knew or in some cases a composite of several Marines, and the same goes for the events. Another way writers develop compelling fictional characters is to conduct an interview with each of them. These writers will compile a dozen or more questions and seriously set out to "interview" each character on elements such as their background, their favorite music, and the name and breed of their favorite family dog. This approach relates to writer Anne Lamott's analogy of providing an emotional acre per character. One writer I know even assigns a birthday to each of his characters so that he can develop his characters' personalities and reactions to conflicts based on traits related to their Zodiac sign. A whole new take on the pickup line *What's your sign?*

Another way of developing believable fictional characters is to study archetypes. *Archetype* comes from the Greek word *archetypo*, meaning "first of its kind." When we think of archetypes, we tend to leap toward the familiar one of a hero on a journey. It's safe to say every protagonist, including you if you're writing memoir, is on a journey of sorts in the most compelling storytelling. By the end of a story the protagonist, or those around him or her, undergoes a transformation. If the journey doesn't reveal a deeper understanding or spark new reflections for our protagonist, then we aren't providing much reward for our reader.

Tami D. Cowden offers another interesting approach to uncovering character in her book *The Complete Writer's Guide to Heroes and Heroines: Sixteen Master Archetypes.* Cowden breaks down the interesting components of behavior behind male archetypes such as the Lost Soul, the Chief, the Bad Boy, and the Warrior. Consider what story conflicts you could create for Cowden's archetypal Bad Boy, whom she describes as the boy who always knows the friend in the right place for creating the not-so-right shortcut. The Bad Boy, however, burns every bridge. He is formed, according to Cowden, "by secrets from his past."

Armed with this information, what circumstances might you create for your fictional military bad boy? What demons from his childhood, for example, would spill into, and maybe ruin, his ability to lead a military unit? Do you allow him moments of grace during which he will change and overcome his past?

Do you sense the levels of possible conflict he might face? Here we're storytelling on several conflict levels: the person versus himself; the person versus another person; and a hint, so far, of the person versus society, for our protagonist will no doubt have to conform, at least somewhat, to society's expectations if he is to overcome the demons from his past.

Or perhaps he won't conform at all. If this sounds contradictory, suppose your bad boy military protagonist survives what others cannot *because* of his streetwise skills born from a childhood of neglect or abuse. And the protagonist experiences an epiphany, or realization. What will he do now, armed with this realization? Will he be able to let go of the anger that has caused him in the past to burn every bridge? Will he try to walk a different path, stumble backward along the way, and try again? Will you allow him to succeed in the end? Or will he fail, despite his best efforts at finding redemption?

A word of caution here: if you use archetypal traits to define your characters, guard against writing stereotypes: the overbearing, overconfident second lieutenant or the crusty E-9, for example. If your characters present a few stereotypical traits, then delve deeper to present a surprising backstory for how they became who and what they are. What is the lieutenant really hiding underneath that overbearing attitude? What military experiences have led the E-9 to be crusty? What surprisingly tender memories does the E-9 reflect upon in quiet moments?

Whatever circumstances you create for your protagonist, remember that the reader is hungry for a deeper connection and understanding of the human condition, Faulkner's "human heart in conflict with itself." Whether writing fiction or memoir, even poetry for that matter, the most compelling storytelling goes far beyond the events themselves and stirs an emotional response within your reader, who is along on the journey with the protagonist and likely pondering what he or she would do under the same set of circumstances.

Suppose your protagonist is one of Cowden's archetypal heroines. In her book Cowden divulges behavioral components of archetypes behind labels such as the Boss, the Librarian, and the Seductress. The

Librarian character, for example, is classified as someone "controlled and clever, she holds back." Can you imagine a military scenario that would include a character with these traits? Even more important would be her backstory, for she wasn't born being controlled and clever; she wasn't born with the sense that she needs to hold back to protect herself. So, what in her background shaped these traits, and how do they influence her current choices?

What happens when Cowden's Bad Boy archetype meets her Librarian archetype? The Bad Boy, according to Cowden, sees the Librarian as a "know-it-all . . . a challenge." The Librarian sees the Bad Boy as "crass . . . able to bring out her wild side." While these reactions may feel stereotypical at first, the real challenge is presenting interesting dilemmas that will stretch both characters. Cowden illustrates the Bad Boy / Librarian interaction with the movie 9½ Weeks.

3. *Person versus nature*: This category of conflict pits the protagonist against nearly unbearable natural elements, such as the sea, a hurricane, or the heat of the desert. When I finally made it to Twentynine Palms to cover that regiment's training exercise, the temperatures were well over one hundred degrees. The men had had a week to acclimate; I hit the ground running, so to speak, recording interviews and clicking off photographs for the base newspaper and beyond. I became dehydrated and grew sicker every day. But I kept pressing on, and in writing about this conflict in my memoir, I hoped to give the reader a sense of what it was like to be a woman during that era—a woman who had little choice but to play the martyr.

Here's a passage infused with sensory language that depicts a challenge against nature in "To Iraq," which appears in *Shade It Black: Death and After in Iraq* by Jessica Goodell and John Hearn:

> We couldn't identify the smell or locate its source, but eventually realized that it had to come from the land itself. It was the smell of a countryside without infrastructure, without piping, plumbing, or treatment plants. It was the smell of soil gone old and decrepit, ground that had lost its nutrients hundreds of years ago. There were cows in the field in the direction I was facing and they were

emaciated, because the grass had dried up into something that even hungry cows would not eat . . . They looked lost too and as out of place as the man I had seen wandering the desert, or the occasional house we passed, stuck in the sand, without a yard, a neighborhood, or a nearby town. As lost and as out of place as we must have looked.

4. *Person versus society and ideas:* I hinted at this final category of conflict when I told about portraying life for a woman Marine during an era even less favorable to women than today's. The era during which your military story takes place offers a plethora of cultural and historical reference possibilities. In *Eyes Right*, for example, I depict the prevailing attitudes of the Cold War era. Whatever the era, details such as musical references, the cost of gasoline, maybe the make and model of your first car or what you paid for it—all these are details that help portray society and societal concepts and thereby lend credibility to your story. In the earlier passage from "To Iraq," Goodell and Hearn convey a striking cultural and societal image in the sentence that begins, "It was the smell of countryside without infrastructure . . ."

Kim Wright's humorous essay about her father's IQ genius also hints at this fourth type of conflict: her father's worry about measuring up against a society that holds the educated and advantaged in higher esteem. Other examples might include a gay soldier who struggles against bigotry, a sailor who refuses to participate in traditional hazing practices aboard ship, or an Air Force chaplain who practices Islam.

You may have noticed that several of these examples actually reveal multiple levels of conflict, all happening, or nearly so, at the same time. The more levels of conflict, the more a character's depth is revealed, including your own if you are writing memoir. All character—yours or that of a fictional protagonist—is revealed by the choices one makes when faced with conflict.

In his first memoir, *Jarhead*, Anthony Swofford writes about having contemplated suicide and the distraction presented by his friend Troy. How many levels of conflict do you notice in just this one short passage?

> Perhaps I wouldn't have pulled the trigger. Maybe Troy's good timing saved me. I think about my sister, this very minute living in an institution in California, and I consider myself a poor imposter, an actor speaking the wrong lines. I don't know what I want, but obviously I don't want badly enough to be dead. I think about Hemingway. What a shot. What despair. What courage. Some insist that the suicide is both a coward and a cheat, but I think the suicide is rather courageous. To look at one's life and decide that it's not worth living, then to go through with the horrible act. Millions of people live lives that aren't worth living. Many fewer people end their worthless lives. To look down the barrel of the gun or over the lip of the pill bottle and say, "That is what I want, that is the world that needs me, better than breath, better than banging my bones through the remainder of these sorry days"—there is the courageous man and woman, the suicide.
>
> But I don't own the courage to kill myself. I must return to the thing I know best, possibly the only thing I truly know: being a jarhead.

Let's imagine conflict as a four-way intersection you or your fictional character has reached. You're facing three choices, four if you turn around and backtrack. The choice you take reveals your character, at least your character at that moment in life, and your character has been shaped by all the moments that have come before it. In other words, at our theoretical intersection of life, is this the moment you, or your protagonist, chooses to turn right after a lifetime of left turns? If so, why? What has changed in your life, or the life of your fictional protagonist, that compels a different course this time? Our readers aren't likely to accept that one day we woke up and arbitrarily decided to make a right turn.

Writing Project

Glancing back at your freewriting Journal Entries 9 and 10 regarding pivotal moments along your timeline, choose three entries and identify the nature of the conflict(s) involved in each one. Thinking back to those events, how many levels of conflict could you expose if you were to write about each event as memoir? If instead you were to fictionalize each event, what levels of conflict do you think you would need to add? Provide details about the additional levels of conflict and how you think they would be useful in telling a more dramatic story.

JOURNAL ENTRY 14

If you're a veteran, locate your DD-214 (military discharge papers) to help jog your memory and recall triggering incidents that you can use for writing nonfiction or fiction. (If you're not a veteran, locate your family member's DD-214 or other military paperwork, such as citations or copies of orders, or an obituary that might provide information about your loved one's military service.) Two decades after my discharge, I realized that I'd misplaced my DD-214 during one of my many moves. When a replacement finally arrived from Kansas City, I was stunned by all that I'd forgotten. Each item on that DD-214 offered an opening into a new writing opportunity.

Choose one thing—say that time you were stationed aboard that LST or that time you received office hours and a bust in rank because you were late returning from the best weekend of your life in Tijuana. Or maybe you were supposed to wash your co's car and wrecked it on the way back—that's a true story from someone I know. Freewrite for twenty to thirty minutes. Write down the bones: the who, what, where, when, how, and why. We'll return later in another writing project to flesh out the rest, such as the emotional aspects behind each experience.

JOURNAL ENTRY 15

From your selected military reading, what levels of conflict can you already identify? What keeps you turning the page? What are you hungry to know about the story, its characters, and their choices during conflicts?

Note: Keep reading to the end of your military selection!

JOURNAL ENTRY 16

Let's pause for a little meaningful self-reflection. Record your thoughts to this question: *In what ways have your ideals about writing been supported or challenged at this point?*

6

Shaping Our Storytelling with Structure

The goal, I suppose, any fiction writer has, no matter what your subject,

is to hit the human heart and the tear ducts and the nape of the neck

and to make a person feel something about what the characters are

going through and to experience the moral paradoxes and struggles of

being human. —TIM O'BRIEN

So far, we've worked on identifying our military story possibilities. We've created a personal timeline of pivotal moments, and from these moments we've contemplated how the four levels of conflict affect each one. We've identified ourselves as the protagonist of our own life story—for those of us writing memoir—and by reviewing the levels of conflict, we've also begun to identify the antagonists of our life story. What our readers will want to know is not only why we feel and act the way we do during those conflicts but why we think or feel our antagonist is reacting in a certain way. We may not ever truly know why the antagonists in our lives are motivated to do what they do, but revealing to our readers that now, looking back, we're attempting to answer those questions provides them with a much more contemplative, rewarding story. As memoirist Patricia Hampl famously claims, "You give me your story, I get mine." Maybe this explains why we're so drawn to true-life stories, or at least to the good parts where the human heart is in conflict with itself, for in doing so, writer and reader are making a most profoundly human connection with one another.

For those of us writing fiction, we're hopefully beginning to imagine more clearly a fictional protagonist and antagonist; ideas for conflicts are also beginning to form. Maybe our storytelling will be based on true events but will be reimagined in a way that only we can do because we're beginning to answer such questions as *What if this happened to my protagonist? How would he or she feel? How would he or she react—and how are these reactions based on previous experiences from his or her life?* Just as important, we are beginning to examine why our antagonist might cause such conflicts for our protagonist. What experiences from his or her life compel such conflict, for unlike memoirists who work from assumptions until or unless we gain a confession from our antagonists, the fiction writer will need to understand the motives of the antagonist as clearly as he or she understands those of the protagonist.

Robert McKee, in his book *Story: Substance, Structure, Style, and the Principles of Screenwriting*, makes a point about the principle of antagonism: "A protagonist and his story can only be as intellectually fascinating and emotionally compelling as the forces of antagonism make them."

Fiction writers get to make up these forces of antagonism, and by "forces" I'm not just referring to the creation of villains. Certainly, an antagonist can have villainous tendencies, but remember our four levels of conflict. Forces of antagonism may also spring from within our protagonist. One force of antagonism could be an act of nature such as a sudden dust storm in the desert that threatens the mission.

Memoir writers, on the other hand, don't get to make up the forces of antagonism, except when sharing with their readers what they imagined as the motives for the antagonists in their lives, and I encourage memoirists to examine, thoroughly and honestly, the self-generated choices we, as the protagonists of our memoirs, make while responding to various forces of antagonism; if there's no brave revelation forthcoming from us, there's likely little reward for our readers. While writing *Eyes Right*, I often hesitated about revealing the most troubling aspects of who I was in my twenties. Looking back now with the gift of time and maturity, I feel great sympathy for that twenty-something self. In the end I knew that if I were to tell the most complete story of my time in the Marines, I'd have to reveal who I really was then. Before the memoir's release, I flew from Florida to California to discuss the book's tough topics with my daughter, Morgan, who at the time was in her mid-twenties. We were dining at our favorite Santa Monica restaurant when I revealed the details about why I had joined the Marines and, even more important, why I left. I watched her process the truth—my version of the truth, anyway, for I was certain her father might have a different version. But then she pointed a finger straight at me. "Mom," she said, looking so much like the old me, or rather the young me, "you have to tell this story." And I did.

Writer and professor Pinckney Benedict feels the choice of writing our experiences as fiction or nonfiction doesn't have to be either/or. He believes we can do both. "The happy thing about being a writer is, you don't use up source material by writing about it. You can take a single incident, a single image, a single moment, and render it as fiction, nonfiction, poetry, a painting, a comic book, a blog. Each incarnation will be something new. Every time you examine your own experience with the idea of rendering it as a work of art, you'll unfold aspects of it that went previously undiscovered and that are particular to that version of it. One expression of it might be superior to another, but none of them will be invalid."

However you decide to express yourself within your writing—through fiction or nonfiction—I'd encourage you to consider this: *What's in this for me, and what's in this for my reader?*

One of the greatest challenges for any writer, new or experienced, is where to start the story because every story has a life that existed before the opening sentence and that will exist after the final sentence, unless you kill off everyone in the final scene (and by doing so you risk stirring hatred within your reader for providing an unimaginative ending). Kurt Vonnegut states in his "Eight Basics of Creative Writing" that we should "start as close to the end as possible."

I followed Vonnegut's advice while crafting *Eyes Right*. I open the memoir with a scene that takes place during the final weeks of my life as a Marine. In the opening I'm following a sergeant from Military Police down a long, polished corridor to a room where I will be the subject of an investigation for a number of charges that are likely to lead to a court-martial. After the opening scene, during which I ground the reader in time and place and give a sense of how much time has passed since the day of interrogation at Military Police headquarters, I circle back to childhood and then through my earliest years as a Marine—all with the goal of leading the reader back to the interrogation room at Military Police headquarters. The structure of *Eyes Right*, if illustrated, might look something like this:

> > > > > > >VVVVVVVVVV> > > > > > > >VVVVVVVVVVVVVVVV> > > > > > > >VVVVVV

Interrogation—Childhood—Interrogation—Marine experiences—Interrogation—Resolution

Where we don't start a story is with the weather. This type of opening is considered clichéd. "It was a dark and stormy night" has already been taken, parodied, and buried in storyland history.

Most writers agree that the best start is to drop a reader into the middle of an action that involves a character. This technique is called "in medias res," from the Latin for "into the midst of things." The opening action is often referred to as the triggering incident, or the inciting incident. William Faulkner once reported that it was the single mental image of a character's muddy underpants that inspired his novel *The Sound and the Fury*.

The inciting incident is usually our way into a story. For some of us, as for Faulkner, the inciting incident could be born from an image or a memory or an overheard conversation. In *An Unlawful Order* I use an event from real life—a fatal helicopter crash that occurred in the 1980s, while I was the public affairs officer on the New River Air Station in North Carolina. That day, which was Columbus Day, should have been a day off work for me, but something told me to go into the office while my husband was playing golf and to use the quiet hours to catch up on paperwork. Moments later the phone rang with the horrific news that we'd lost a helicopter and nineteen Marines when the bird went down five miles off the coast during a routine training exercise with the Navy.

I used bits and pieces of the actual event to form the opening of my novel. From memory I was able to reconstruct how my protagonist would feel and how she would react to the news. Because I was writing a work of fiction, however, I was able to expand and collapse actual events as I desired.

During my opening chapter I drop the reader into the mind of a grieving Capt. Chase Anderson, public affairs officer, on one of her grueling runs around the base on Hawaii. The reader learns in just a few paragraphs that she is a mother to a five-year-old and that she is grieving the loss of her Marine husband to a helicopter crash in Afghanistan. Before the end of page 1 her sergeant drives up and announces the news of a helicopter crash and the nineteen lost Marines during a training exercise with the Navy five miles off the coast of Hawaii. He informs her that all the media are gathering at the gate for her statement. Can you sense the rising tension and conflicts? Capt. Chase Anderson jumps into action, and we begin to discover details about her character by the choices she makes under pressure that day.

I have never lost a husband in a helicopter crash in Afghanistan, and the event that I'm referencing happened decades before the one I re-create for my novel. But can you see how I've drawn from personal experience and expanded the story for the sake of creating a larger, more thought-provoking narrative than what actually happened on a single, yet tragic, day during my own military career?

Also, did you notice that I drop my readers smack into the middle of the action? From the outset my readers are quickly able to identify the protagonist, the setting, Hawaii, and a story conflict, the helicopter crash and the fact that Capt. Chase Anderson will have to face the media.

Let's take a look at the opening of Ernest Hemingway's military novel *For Whom the Bell Tolls*: "He lay flat on the brown, pine-needled floor of the forest, his chin on his folded arms, and high overhead the wind blew in the tops of the pine trees. The mountainside sloped gently where he lay; but below it was steep and he could see the dark of the oiled road winding through the pass. There was a stream alongside the road and far down the pass he saw a mill beside the stream

and the falling water of the dam, white in the summer sunlight."
What we don't know yet is *why* Hemingway's protagonist, who he'll
eventually reveal as Robert Jordan, is there on the mountainside,
looking down. But we're curious. We're in the middle of the scene
with Hemingway's character, and what we'll discover within a page or
two is that Robert Jordan is there to plant explosives in order to blow
up a bridge. Hemingway could have opened his novel with a scene
depicting Jordan actually planting explosives, but instead, Hemingway drops us beside Jordan on that mountainside. He does this, I
believe, to ignite our curiosity and to begin ratcheting up suspense
and tension so that we will be compelled to read on.

As part of the architecture of storytelling, a writer builds a story
based on progressive complications. By progressive complications,
I'm referring to a series of answers that satisfy readers' questions
of "and then what happened?" Let's say conflict A affects our protagonist . . . *and then what happens?* Our protagonist makes a choice
when presented with the conflict . . . *and then what happens?* Will
our protagonist's choice lead to destructive consequences? Cause and
effect, action and reaction. As readers, we're eager to learn about the
consequences of characters' actions.

If readers are satisfied, they will eagerly turn page after page to
uncover the progressive complications we have depicted. Each com-
plication for our protagonist should increase, at least slightly, in intensity. Building the intensity builds drama and tension.

This is where an understanding of the four levels of conflict comes
in handy. Perhaps you've decided to land your reader in the middle
of a conflict that pits one person against another. Perhaps your protagonist will next confront a conflict involving a person versus nature
or a person versus him- or herself.

Simply put, our goal as writers is to guide our readers from page 1
to the end. The best way to do this is to keep our readers engaged. The
best way to engage our readers is to expose our characters to credible
dilemmas or obstacles predicated on their goals, needs, and yearnings
and then to expose the emotional motivations behind the actions they
take to overcome, or not overcome, the obstacles (see tip 1).

Thinking about progressive complications, let's pretend for a moment that we're writing a short story about a young man who joins the military just to anger his parents and rebel against a father's authority. Suppose, instead, that his parents praise him for enlisting. They praise his courage. Stunned by this reaction, how will our young character react now? What are the consequences of his parents' praise and of his decision to join the military to spite them? Will we allow him to have regrets for his impulsive enlistment? What will those regrets look like? Will he voice them through dialogue to a girlfriend or a buddy? Will he shout obscenities at his parents, walk out, and never return? What if we were to allow his parents' praise for his courage to compel him, instead, toward ridiculously heroic risks during combative conditions because he thinks he now has to live up to that praise?

Suppose we ratchet up the tension even more. What if our protagonist's risk taking were to cause the death of his best friend, *and* what if our character is nonetheless heralded as a hero, despite the outcome? How will he deal with all this? How will he reckon with the truth, even if he is the only one who knows the whole truth? How will he respond to his parents after the homecoming when they continue to praise him for his courage? Does he blame them for setting him on this particular course? Does he ever take responsibility for his own motivations and actions? And if he does, how? Or instead of a how, maybe it's a *who*—someone new in his life who leads him to self-discovery or further self-destruction.

Marine veteran Thomas Vincent Nowaczyk addresses what he strives for in his military storytelling. "The thing I am trying to do most in my writing is to convey the emotion attached to experience, experiential validity in art, if you will. Anything that allows me to amp up how emotionally invested the reader becomes in the story is good."

Another tool for building your story is through character development. Many new writers believe this begins by determining the physical characteristics: blond hair, blue eyes, wiry build. Physical characteristics are helpful but overrated. What we remember even more, as readers, are those specific details that we simply can't shake about a character. Years after publishing a somewhat humorous essay about an ex-husband's facelift, for example, I continue to hear from readers about a particular line of character development—"the man who would not let me eat Chinese food more than once a year"— because this description was juxtaposed with his sudden desire to undergo a risky full facelift.

Let's suppose we have a character who is a chain smoker. We'll plant details about cigarettes or smoking along the way, like bread-crumbs, and that detail of character will pay off somehow in the end.

Another way to reveal character is through dialogue. What we say, the way we use vocabulary and the way we form sentences, reveals a great deal about us and our characters. In the same facelift essay I refer to the Belgian doctor's heavy accent and prolific use of car analogies: "You're no Porsche yet, but you looking good, Vincent" and "Don't get too cocky, Crow. You're still a used Cadillac."

Think all Americans speak alike? Hardly. So, it's a good idea to keep in mind the dialect associated with the region of the country in which your character has either grown up or lived a significant number of years. In North Carolina, for example, a refrigerator was an icebox, at least to my grandparents. I think I always reverted back to icebox whenever I visited as an adult. In all my childhood homes we sat on couches, not sofas. My grandmother's temporary fix to a falling blind was "scotched" in place.

If you're writing a fictional military story, you can obviously choose the region from which your characters will hail. And if your military story ties several characters to one military unit, say in Afghanistan, you'll want to determine the childhood background for each charac-ter and their childhood influences. Create a character profile, includ-ing key vocabulary words. As you prepare lines of dialogue for each character, be sure to sprinkle in the region-specific dialect.

But the truest way to reveal character is by showing the reader how and why the character makes certain choices during times of conflict. There's that key word again: *conflict.*

Your readers will be eager to learn why your character chooses to turn left in life rather than right. Or why your character is choosing revenge over forgiveness, or vice versa. And this also applies to those who plan to pen a military memoir. During a one-on-one meeting after a writing workshop with the incredible writing instructor and author Michael Steinberg, he said he hoped I would eventually reveal how my relationship with my father had influenced my career-ending decision to have an affair with a well-known Marine Corps general. I was blown away. Steinberg had only read the opening chapter, which at the time merely hinted at my father's fatal car accident when I was twenty. As Steinberg handed over the chapter, I realized that at forty-six I hadn't even considered examining my father's death and its overarching influence. But I knew in that moment of the meeting with Steinberg that I would and that my memoir would be significantly and permanently changed, as would I.

Every story is also told from a point of view (POV), meaning from whose perspective or voice the story is being told. If you're writing about your own military experiences and plan to tell them truthfully in a memoir, then you will be telling your story from what's called the first-person POV. When you are writing memoir, *you* are the protagonist of your own life story. Don't confuse protagonist with hero, however. Being the protagonist doesn't mean you get to come out on top of every conflict, unless, of course, that's true—even so, I'm afraid, your readers will quickly tire of your grandiosity and self-worshipping.

Within our lives are the people with whom we have been influenced or challenged or betrayed, and while those folks may become characters on the pages of our memoirs, they are most important for how they shaped who we are today.

So, your memoir may reveal a Broadway play cast of memorable characters who have moved in and out of your life, but you are still the protagonist, and the reader is most interested in how *you* think you've been shaped by the cast of characters.

Here, for example, is the opening to my memoir, *Eyes Right*.

When I was twenty-eight, younger than my daughter is today, I was facing the likelihood of a court-martial. I followed a Marine sergeant down a polished corridor, past the clacking of typewriters and murmurs behind the closed doors of Military Police Headquarters, and pretended to be unafraid, as if I had nothing to hide, as if on the way there that morning I hadn't seriously mapped out a plan for desertion. Inhaling and exhaling in the same forced rhythm of a runner pacing through a psychological wall, I was committed to a marathon of sorts, and so I was breathing in and breathing out, matching foot speed and cadence with the young Marine ahead of me: a machinated force, we were, matching left foot and right, left arm and right, until he pulled up short in front of a closed door. My toe stubbed against the heel of his boot. Acting politely unaware, he pushed open the door and stepped aside for me to enter. He wore well his role of consummate Marine, refusing the eye contact I was desperate to interpret.

"The captain will be with you shortly, Ma'am," he said.

I forced a smile. "Thank you, Sergeant." After he disappeared behind the closed door, I heard those machine-like limbs working their way back down the corridor.

In creating this opening, I had two primary goals: to ground my reader in time and place and to hook my reader by quickly establishing a sense of conflict. Notice the "I" voice, for I am the narrator of my own story.

Here's a scene from Pulitzer Prize–winning writer and Vietnam veteran Tracy Kidder's essay "War Stories," which appears in the anthology *Red, White, and True* and is excerpted from his book-length memoir about his time in Vietnam, *My Detachment*. Besides the use of "I" as first-person POV, notice the levels of conflict and Kidder's use of sensory details.

A mortar round went overhead. In the silence that followed, I heard a banging at my screen door. I looked up and saw Pancho saunter in. I was in my underwear. He was fully dressed, still wearing his sunglasses. "Hi," I said, brushing away the mosquito net. I swung my legs over the side of the cot. "Can I help you?"

He sat down on my footlocker and said, very calmly, "Lieutenant, you know what a lifer is? You know what a lifing, begging puke is, Lieutenant?"

"What?"

He went right on. "It's a flatdick who lifes and begs and pukes all over EM scum, Lieutenant. Ain't like a man, Lieutenant."

The Army had films and pamphlets to instruct a soldier in all the activities of daily living, and I had gone to training camps for over a year and learned to avoid venereal disease and march and make my bed and fire weapons, but I had never received a single instruction in how to handle troops. I remembered how, during her first year of teaching high school, my mother would come home almost every day in tears. The Army should have sent me to an inner-city high school for six months and let me try to keep order in the cafeteria. As it was, I had an idea that being an officer, I would be obeyed. I didn't know exactly what this short kid in dark glasses was talking about, but I could tell it was impertinent and I shouldn't put up with it. I said, "Now wait a minute, Specialist."

Pancho said, "We don't like some of the things you're doing around here, Lieutenant."

"Well, that's too bad," I said.

"We can shoot you any time we want, Lieutenant," he said.

"Oh, yeah?"

"Yeah, Lieutenant. We can."

"I'll shoot you first, asshole," I said to him, but under my breath and after he'd gone and I was sitting on my cot under a bare light bulb, and staring out toward the dark. The light reached only a few yards beyond my rusty screen walls. I couldn't see out, but anyone could stand in the patch of tall grass near my hootch and see my lighted silhouette.

The first-person POV isn't just for memoirists, however. Short story writers and novelists also employ first-person POV when they want to present a story from a single character's mind-set and through his or her observations. Notice I used the words *single* and *mind-set*? First-person POV can be limiting. You are trapping your reader inside the mental and emotional intelligence of a single character. Think back to the opening of my memoir. I've trapped my reader inside my head as I walk the long hallway to the interrogation room. Sure, there's a Marine sergeant leading the way, but what do you know about him? Only what I'm telling you, that he appears the consummate professional despite the indignity associated with an interrogation of a Marine Corps officer.

Some readers profess to love the "I" voice for its sense of intimacy, even in short stories and novels. *Pull up a chair*, this POV seems to project, *and I'll tell you a story.* Here's an example of that intimate, storytelling voice from the opening of Kurt Vonnegut's *Slaughterhouse-Five*: "All this happened, more or less. The war parts, anyway, are pretty much true. One guy I knew really *was* shot in Dresden for taking a teapot that wasn't his. Another guy I knew really *did* threaten to have his personal enemies killed by hired gunmen after the war. And so on. I've changed all the names."

Here's another example of first-person POV in a short story by Marine veteran Kevin C. Jones, "The Edge of Water," which appears in the collection *Home of the Brave: Somewhere in the Sand.* You're likely to notice that the voice is less conversational yet still intimate. The prose is lyrical, even musical, thanks to Jones's artful technique of using repetition: "That November after Iraq, after all the surgeries on my leg, after I could get around with crutches instead of a wheelchair, after the bruising was only a memory and the concussion toned down to a few, minor headaches that only bothered me in bright sunlight or movie theatres, I found myself in California again."

The challenge for writer and reader with first-person POV is that everything we learn about secondary characters will be filtered through the mind of the narrator. Of course, what the narrator *chooses* to relate about secondary and tertiary characters is also quite revealing about the narrator—ourselves, in the case of memoir—so you'll want to keep those choices in mind as you develop your narrator's single POV. I like what writer Anne Lamott states about characters in her essay "Shitty First Drafts": "Each of your characters has an emotional acre that they tend, or don't tend." As a writer, discover what each character's emotional acre looks like.

Writers have other POV choices. Second-person POV, which is projected through the pronoun *you*, is an option but often reads as too gimmicky. So, why would a writer choose this POV? Because it allows for a certain amount of distance between the narrator and the subject matter. Even though I just allotted a fair amount of space to explaining how memoirists write in first-person POV, I can also make an argument for switching to second-person. The effect is sometimes jarring and off-putting for the reader, so it should be carefully rendered. The second-person POV often works best for short sections. My memoir, for example, includes a single chapter all written in second-person POV because I wanted to portray a different voice for my reader. Here's a brief segment of a chapter revealing my reactions after being lost during the night compass test for officers at Quantico:

> You read somewhere that scientists believe the magnetic poles reverse themselves every five hundred thousand years or so— meaning what is north today flips south tomorrow—and since Earth is apparently long overdue for a reversal of magnetic poles . . . suppose your compass needle has been pointing south all along? . . . Then you stuff the map and compass into your field jacket pocket, make a half turn toward the direction from where you came, and walk on, just walking, no longer thinking or caring about step counts and meters, for what does all that matter if your whole world has turned upside down.

I purposely chose second-person POV here because in my mind this change of voice from first-person to second-person portrays the surreal out-of-body sense of isolation for the narrator, me, who is terrified about failing the night compass test. But as you can imagine, this point of view, as with first-person, is also quite limiting. The reader is once again trapped in a single mind-set.

Arguably, the most common and natural form of storytelling is through the use of third-person POV. Maybe we find this version of storytelling so comfortable because it's most often used in the classical fairy tales on which we were weaned. This POV enables us to feel as if we're a fly on the wall, watching, observing the scenes unfold, though in third-person POV we're watching them filtered through the eyes of a single narrator. Here's an example of third-person POV from Laura Hillenbrand's biography *Unbroken: A World War II Story of Survival, Resilience, and Redemption*:

> In the predawn darkness of August 26, 1929, in the back bedroom of a small house in Torrance, California, a twelve-year-old boy sat up in bed, listening. There was a sound coming from outside, growing ever louder. It was a huge, heavy rush, suggesting immensity, a great parting of air. It was coming from directly above the house. The boy swung his legs off his bed, raced down the stairs, slapped open the back door, and loped onto the grass. The yard was otherworldly, smothered in unnatural darkness, shivering with sound. The boy stood on the lawn beside his older brother, head thrown back, spellbound.

You can see that in this example of third-person POV we are still only getting one perspective; it is a static third-person perspective. We don't know, for instance, what the brother is thinking. We don't know if he was awakened by the same noises or if he'd been standing outside all along.

Here's another example, taken from the short story "The Things He Saw," by David Abrams, in *Home of the Brave: Somewhere in the Sand*. Notice the details we're learning about the protagonist and those around him through the eyes of Abrams's protagonist, who is an army photographer in Iraq:

> If he could go back there to the belly of that plane and say one thing to those soldiers, humid with their fears and bravado, he'd

tell Dietrich to relax, to loosen the death grip on his rifle. He'd tell all of them none of it mattered, not in the long run.

Dietrich would be gone in just under a month. All four limbs simultaneously amputated in a blizzard of shrapnel from a roadside bomb. He only has one other photo of Dietrich, but this is the one he prefers, the one where you can see his knuckles.

Besides first-, second-, and third-person POVs, writers may also choose a variation of third-person, known as the omniscient narrator. Think of this point of view as truly godlike, for writers using this point of view jump from the mind of one character to that of another. Doing so allows the reader to know everything about the characters, such as how they think and why each chooses to respond to conflict in the ways they do. In other words, no more limitations, as you'll see in this short example of omniscient narration from Tim O'Brien's *The Things They Carried*: "They imagined the muzzle against flesh. So easy: squeeze the trigger and blow away a toe. They imagined it. They imagined the quick, sweet pain, then the evacuation to Japan, then a hospital with warm beds and cute geisha nurses."

For a while omniscient narration appeared to have fallen out of favor with the writing world. As with any profession, trends come and go. In fact, students of writing programs—so unfamiliar today with the kind of omniscient narration that dominated literature in the Victorian era—sometimes have trouble recognizing this point of view and call out another writer for having made rookie errors in properly establishing point of view.

Yes, we've come to accept that the majority of stories we read today will be told through devices of first- or third-person point of view. But as long as the reader is comfortably grounded within each character's mind-set, a jump in mind-set shouldn't be so jarring that it negatively affects the reader's experience. Consider scenes in David Abrams's critically acclaimed military novel, *Fobbit*, during which he assumes the point of view of two nonhuman characters—an EOD robot in the VBIED standoff and the descending mortar en route to kill one of the book's characters. As Abrams explains, "Writing from the perspective of a machine felt fresh to me."

In the short story "The World, the Flesh, and the Devil" Pinckney Benedict alternates between the points of view of a downed military aviator and a wild dog that is chasing the aviator. Here's a short passage from the dog's POV: "He shoved his way forward in the pack, striving for all he was worth, until there were no dogs in front of him. He flew through the forest, and the frontrunner's howl broke from his throat, and the dogs behind him took it up, adding their voices to the awful wail."

How will you know which point of view works best? If you're writing memoir, the answer is simple, of course: mostly first-person POV. If you're writing fiction, I suggest you choose the POV that feels most natural to you and remain open-minded to other possibilities (see tip 2).

When I was in the earliest stages of drafting my novel, *An Unlawful Order*, for example, I struggled with the same opening pages for weeks. Something kept preventing me from being able to advance the story, yet I couldn't identify that *something*. I certainly knew what life was like for a Marine Corps public affairs officer, and since I was drawing on personal experience of being the public affairs officer for an air station on the day of a tragic helicopter crash, I certainly understood what was at stake for my protagonist, Capt. Chase Anderson, during those initial pages. For all these reasons I had logically chosen to write the novel from Chase Anderson's first-person POV—her "I" voice.

One day I casually mentioned to my writer friend Jeffery Hess that I was stuck in the first chapter and couldn't understand why. "Chase Anderson is a version of you," he said, "but she's not you." He reminded me of my memoir background, which focused on the truthful rendering of fact and memory through my "I" voice. "Switch to third-person POV," he said, "and see if that helps."

Could it really be that simple?

Yes. I rewrote those opening pages from Chase's third-person POV and immediately sensed the freedom to stray as far as I wanted and needed from the restricting facts of the actual helicopter crash and my role as the public affairs officer on that fateful day, and I finished the first draft of the novel in less than four months.

Writing Project

JOURNAL ENTRY 17

Answer these questions about your writing so far:

> I want to write a military story about _____.
> What makes me most nervous about telling this story is _____.
> The reason I have to tell this story is _____.
> What I want readers (or my family, for you memoir writers) to gain from this story is _____.

Choose a pivotal moment from your timeline. It's okay to use the same one that you've been working on in Journal Entries 7 and 8. (If you're a veteran, consider choosing something from your DD-214 freewriting project [Journal Entry 14].) If you're writing fiction, let me suggest that you work on this prompt with the story idea that's been forming in your imagination as you've been reading your military selection and working on the writing prompts.

Now, let's do some simple research on the era during which your story takes place. Incorporating historical, political, and cultural references in your storytelling helps the reader feel grounded in time and place. For starters look back on your pivotal storytelling moment and answer the following:

> Who was president of the United States?
> What happened on a day in history during your pivotal storytelling moment? What happened in history the day before that pivotal moment? How about in the weeks and months that followed?

What was number 1 on the Billboard charts? Country music
   charts?
What was the postage rate to mail a letter?
What was the number 1 show on television?
What was the number 1 movie in theaters?

JOURNAL ENTRY 18

Using one of the freewriting scenes from your timeline, alter the POV.
If you're writing memoir, rewrite the opening in second- or third-
person. Read it aloud.

   If you prefer, use the fictional scene from Journal Entry 10 and
change the POV; read it aloud. Do you hear the difference?

   Now, let's go even further. Whether you're writing memoir or fiction, for the sake of this writing project, pretend you can enter the
minds of everyone in your scene. What, for example, was your mother
thinking when you told her you were joining the military? Even if you
don't know, allow your imagination to stretch by practicing omniscient narration. If you are writing memoir, here's an example for
how you could later convert this omniscient exercise into your own
POV: "I could tell from the way my mother sliced into the tomatoes,
the way that she refused to look at me after I'd finally delivered the
news, the way her knife plunged into the flesh of one poor tomato
after another, three more than needed for a salad for two, that she
was thinking how she'd like to kill the recruiter who had visited our
high school or my cousin Johnny for the role he played in talking
me into joining. Or maybe I was wrong. Maybe what she was really
thinking is that . . ."

   In memoir it's perfectly acceptable to portray what you, or your
protagonist, may believe someone is thinking as long as you let your
reader know what you're doing, as in my example of the mother's
reaction. If you're writing fiction, you can do the same thing with
your first- and third-person POV, by the way. The most basic advice
I can give about this is to keep your reader grounded in time, place,
and POV.

Remember that scene you revised for point of view in Journal Entry 17? Try revising the opening paragraphs with a different verb tense. Read aloud. What do you think? Which tense works best? Often writers will complete the first draft of a book manuscript and then play around with point of view and verb tense by revising the opening page or two and reading aloud. Don't be afraid to experiment. After all, a memoir, short story, or novel isn't complete until it's published.

Every writer completes what noted writer Anne Lamott describes in her book *Bird by Bird* as the "shitty first draft":

> The first draft is the child's draft, where you let it all pour out and then let it romp all over the place, knowing that no one is going to see it and that you can shape it later. You just let this childlike part of you channel whatever voices and visions come through and onto the page. If one of the characters wants to say, "Well, so what, Mr. Poopy Pants?" you let her. No one is going to see it. If the kid wants to get into really sentimental, weepy, emotional territory, you let him. Just get it all down on paper, because there may be something great in those six crazy pages that you would never have gotten to by more rational, grown-up means. There may be something in the very last line of the very last paragraph on page six that you just love, that is so beautiful or wild that you now know what you're supposed to be writing about, more or less, or in what direction you might go—but there was no way to get to this without first getting through the first five and a half pages.

Tip 1: In fiction the use of coincidence is seen as too easy and too contrived, as is an ending to a story that includes a hero being saved by a god or gods (*deus ex machina*, "a god from a machine," is the Latin term for this seemingly magical resolution). Sure, life is full of coincidences, but this device works better in the nonfiction genre of biography or memoir because real life does involve coincidence and can't be explained any other way.

Tip 2: Another tool for writers is the choice of verb tense. The most common of verb tenses in storytelling, and the one that reads most naturally for readers, is past tense. I was . . . They were . . . Sergeant Michaels reported . . . Because the story we are telling has already happened, even in the case of short stories or novels, we tend to lean toward and favor the use of past tense.

Some writers use present tense, as I did in my memoir, although it's more of a storytelling gimmick, I think, than a useful strategy. What it does provide is a false hyper-focused sense of reality. I did so because I wanted the reader to feel the same sense of panic that I was feeling as I was feeling it. Remember, however, that present tense is just a tool. When it's overused, it loses effect. Here's an example from *Eyes Right* in which I switch from past tense in sections 1 and 2 to present tense in section 3: "Two weeks later, I'm in this interrogation room at Military Police Headquarters, and the captain has finally turned off the tape recorder. The pages of her legal pad are draped over the top, and she's flipping each sheet backward, scanning, and all of this delay feels intentional. A stalling tactic."

7

Activating Energy Shifts within Our Scenes

When we spend a lifetime trying to distance ourselves from the parts of our lives that don't fit with who we think we're supposed to be, we stand outside of our story and hustle for our worthiness by constantly performing, perfecting, pleasing, and proving. Our sense of worthiness—that critically important piece that gives us access to love and belonging—lives inside of our story. —DR. BRENÉ BROWN

Writers depict conflicts and dilemmas through a series of scenes that are strung, like pearls on a silk strand, from beginning to end. Each scene opens a window into the thoughts and actions of our characters and their choices during conflict. We're probably most familiar with scenes in plays and films that show an action taking place within a single setting. The move from one setting to another is made visible to us.

But in our memoirs or short stories our words must evoke mental images. Like good journalists, we become the eyes and ears for our readers—recording who, what, where, when, how, and why within each scene setting. Are we on a battlefield? In a recruiting office with a group of teenagers who are taking the oath? At an Army base when a father grabs his daughter, who is dressed in combat fatigues, for one more hug before she deploys with her unit to Afghanistan? With the grandfather who has driven his PTSD-suffering grandson to see a therapist at the VA? What will the setting for your scene look like?

But describing what one sees in a scene setting is just one way to evoke a mental image. Let's not leave out the other four senses of sound, smell, taste, and touch. How might we employ several of them as well to better establish a mental vision and emotional reaction for our readers? Perhaps there are sounds that are distracting our characters during the scene, such as explosions, sirens, the shuffling of footsteps behind a door, or bird chirps. In "Hulls in the Water," which appears in *Red, White, and True*, Jeffery Hess uses sound imagery while recalling the day his ship was affected by the outer bands of a typhoon: "The ship groaned and creaked as if it might snap apart. There was no predictable pitch or roll. It was rather like being Yahtzee dice in a half-century-old can, but in slow motion . . . the crashes and tumbling roll of unsecured items knocking about. Shipmates doing the same and cursing afterward."

What smells might we include? Smell is our strongest sense, by the way. Can we evoke the sense of touch for a character? Is there a rock pressing into a character's left kidney, for example, as he waits, stealthily tucked under a large bush, for the all clear? As writer E. L. Doctorow contends, "Good writing is supposed to evoke sensation in the reader—not the fact that it is raining, but the feeling of being rained upon."

Let's look at a brief scene passage from Robert O'Connor's novel, *Buffalo Soldiers*, during which he grounds us in time and place, evokes all five senses, and reveals his character's psychological mind-set:

Outside Manheim, West Germany, you are stationed with the 57th. It is November, and Novembers in Germany remind you of the sadness and despair of a fallen woman. Let us also say we know of your fondness for heroin. You want to get off, and two men in your squad need to shoot up. This is how you do it:

There are three floors to your barracks. You get your main buddy, Stoney, and the two others, Simmons and Cabot. You go to the top floor where there are storage rooms and broom closets. Generally, this is the kind of place to be avoided. It is too quiet here, too lonely, and if the yams catch you napping they might tear you a new asshole just for the hell of it. But with Stoney to protect you, you're not worried.

Because we're writing military stories, our scene settings will incorporate military details, at least enough to build credibility with our readers. Novelist David Abrams believes it's always a challenge to relate military service to readers who have no understanding about life in uniform, especially with the widening divide between those who have served and those who have not. "How do we put that reader in our combat boots? We do it by creating empathy for our characters. We do it through telling details, through universally-relevant stories, and through well-crafted language."

Here's one of my all-time favorite military scenes from Tim O'Brien's "How to Tell a True War Story":

We crossed that river and marched west into the mountains. On the third day, my friend Curt Lemon stepped on a booby-trapped artillery round. He was playing catch with Rat Kiley, laughing, and then he was dead. The trees were thick; it took nearly an hour to cut an LZ for the dustoff.

Later, higher in the mountains, we came across a baby VC water buffalo. What it was doing there I don't know—no farms, no paddies—but we chased it down and, got a rope around it and led it along to a deserted village where we set up for the night. After supper Rat Kiley went over and stroked its nose.

He opened a can of C rations, pork and beans, but the baby buffalo wasn't interested.

Rat shrugged.

He stepped back and shot it through the right front knee.

The animal did not make a sound. It went down hard, then got up again, and Rat took careful aim and shot off an ear. He shot it in the hindquarters and in the little hump at its back. He shot it twice in the flanks. It wasn't to kill; it was to hurt. He put the rifle muzzle up against the mouth and shot the mouth away. Nobody said much. The whole platoon stood there watching, feeling all kinds of things, but there wasn't a great deal of pity for the baby water buffalo. Curt Lemon was dead. Rat Kiley had lost his best friend in the whole world.

Even though this is an excerpt from a work of fiction, we are grounded in time and place because O'Brien masterfully moves us through the scene, moment-by-grizzly-heartbreaking-moment.

Years ago, while working on both a screenplay and my memoir, I discovered screenwriting guru Robert McKee, the author of *Story: Substance, Structure, Style, and the Principles of Screenwriting*. While reading the book is life changing for writers in and of itself, hearing McKee present his theories in person, as I did twice, while you have a screenplay, memoir, or novel rolling around inside your head is even more momentous. The greatest lesson I learned, and the one I most enjoyed sharing with my college creative writing classes, is about energy shifts in scenes and how to determine whether a scene is truly working. You see, screenwriters have a basic rule: if the energy doesn't shift from the beginning to the end of the scene, they cut it. So, what does it mean, an energy shift?

Let's go back and consider O'Brien's excerpt. I haven't provided the entire scene, but there's enough of it, I believe, to help illustrate what McKee was referring to. O'Brien has his men marching west, laughing, goofing off, in the beginning, and then, boom, Lemon is dead. This scene begins with negative energy—something sad, tragic, a downward moment. You could place a negative sign in the page margin. And then, of course, there follows the baby buffalo tragedy. But what truly happens at the end of the scene? Nobody says anything, but everyone's feeling something, maybe vindication in some sad way. The scene begins to take an upward turn, ending on an ever-so-slightly positive note. According to McKee's theory about scene work, the energy shift doesn't have to be a dramatic upswing or downward fall. But something or someone must change by the end of the scene. If nothing or nobody changes and no vital information is shared that affects the outcome of future scenes, then the scene is superfluous and most likely headed to the cutting-room floor.

To help illustrate the principle of energy shifts in scenes, I would have my students mark the beginnings and endings of their scenes with plus and minus signs. If they wind up with a plus-plus or a minus-minus for a scene, then they sharpen their pencils and get back to work on how best to charge the scene, or to paraphrase William Faulkner, they may have to kill off their darling.

This lesson also helps them to see if they've fallen in the trap of habitually writing each scene in the same pattern of plus-minus energy followed by another plus-minus scene followed by yet another plus-minus scene. Too much of this and your reader may begin to feel nauseous riding on your contrived roller coaster; at the least, your reader will have little to look forward to in the scene that follows, being able to guess, even if subconsciously, how the next scene will end. The same caution applies to scenes that always begin with negative energy and end on an upward swing. Guard against anything too predictable. No surprise for the reader could result in a disappointed, even bored, reader.

Often new writers aren't sure how long a scene should be. A scene can be as short as a few sentences or a few paragraphs or as long as several pages. Ultimately, a scene ends when the moment of drama ends, and the moment ends when the mood shifts and the setting changes.

Writing Project
JOURNAL ENTRY 20

Throughout the ages writers have improved their skills by modeling the work of other writers. Take another look at the passage from Robert O'Connor's *Buffalo Soldiers*. In your journal rewrite the passage, replacing each of O'Connor's words with your own—a noun for a noun, a verb for a verb, and so on— using material from your military experience. You can continue the use of his second-person POV if you'd like to experiment with second-person.)Be sure to follow the exact rhythm of O'Connor's sentences too. When you finish, read aloud O'Connor's passage, and then read aloud your own. Do you notice the variation in sentence structure and length and how the ebb and flow infuses a degree of musicality within your writing? Take a moment to reflect and journal about your reactions.

JOURNAL ENTRY 21

Choose a scene or the beginning of a chapter from your selected reading. Does the reading begin on a positive charge of energy or a negative one? What is the ending energy for the scene? Try another scene. Remember, energy shifts are often subtle. A scene might begin on a negative and end on a *slightly* less negative, which is moving the energy toward the plus sign.

Now let's work with the opening of a piece of your work. Carve out a single scene. Maybe you haven't yet perfected it, but you know you have a single moment of drama within the work. Does this moment of drama begin on a plus or negative? Can you see ahead, as a writer, where the scene will end? Will it be on a plus action or negative one? Now write your way from the beginning of the scene toward the end, remembering to build the scene by establishing the setting and grounding your reader in time and place. Don't forget to include sensory details related to sound, sights, tactile, and of course smells. I've found it sometimes helps my writing to think of the scene as if I'm watching it come alive on a movie screen. Doing so allows me to walk my reader moment by moment through the action, permitting my reader to take in the sights, sounds, and smells while developing the all-important conflict, internal and external, of the moment.

JOURNAL ENTRY 22

This is a two-part exercise. Try not to skip ahead until you finish part 1, or you'll prematurely influence your learning outcome.

Part 1: In your journal quickly jot down the first ten words that come to mind. Remember . . . no peeking at part 2!

Part 2: Place a C by each word that evokes a concrete image— something that can be seen, touched, smelled, tasted, or heard. *Bird*, for example, would be considered a concrete image.

Now mark an *A*, for "abstract," by each word that is not a concrete image. *Society* is an abstract word. *Democracy* is abstract.

Now total the columns. If you have more concrete images, you probably lean toward using solid nouns in your writing, which generally leads readers to a more vivid, sensory reading experience. If, however, you have more abstract words, you possibly see the larger picture in situations. This isn't a bad thing; it means you probably lean toward developing themes within your writing. The strongest writers work hard to achieve a balance between the concrete and abstract.

Look at a paragraph of a freewriting exercise from one of your journal entries. Look for your nouns. (Need help remembering how to identify nouns? The general rule regarding nouns is that they are a person, place, or thing.) Label each concrete noun with a C and each abstract noun with an A. How can you convert the A's to more concrete images? How can you deepen the theme within your paragraph without losing the vividness of sensory writing?

Sharing Our Stories—When and How

You don't start out writing good stuff. You start out writing crap and thinking it's good stuff, and then gradually you get better at it. That's why I say one of the most valuable traits is persistence. —OCTAVIA BUTLER

Until now everything you've created has probably been for your eyes only. But let's say that along the way of reading and engaging *On Point* writing projects, you poured your heart into a short military memoir or short story—daring greatly, let's assume, to expose your flaws in that memoir or the flaws of your short story characters. You've spent hours toiling away on the work, remembering to provide your reader with rewards by revealing the motivations behind the decisions you made or those of your fictional characters. The work, you believe, portrays you as the narrator or your fictional protagonist enduring several levels of conflict, and conflicts—the external ones anyway—have been conveyed through a string of scenes that keep your reader grounded in time and place and include just the right amount of military jargon and detail and just enough sensory language to evoke such things as sights, sounds, and smells. You've whittled and honed the work to ensure an arc for the narrator (you) or the protagonist, revealing energy shifts along the way, and ultimately satisfying a reader's curiosity about who has been shaped or altered by what has occurred.

Now you're thinking you're ready to share your work, right? But with whom? Family? Friends?

Not so fast. Often the feedback we get from family and friends—

the judgments we sense from them—can be tougher to swallow than feedback we get from others. Remember that adage about how golfers get better by playing with better golfers? When you reach this phase of your writing, if you're truly serious about getting better as a writer, you want honest, credible feedback, which you can get within a writing workshop environment that's run by a legitimate instructor—someone with teaching and publishing experience.

Workshops vary in style and format, depending on the preferences of the workshop leader. The overall premise is that each writer submits a piece of work for the purpose of gaining feedback from other writers in the workshop and from the instructor. This feedback is meant to be judgment free and to pertain only to the writer's techniques. The workshop leader will ask her group to concentrate feedback on such things as how the writer handles dialogue, scene and plot development, and the use of sensory language.

The leader and the others will also examine whether what's at stake for your characters regarding their goals, needs, and desires is clearly defined and whether the stakes rise through more than one level of conflict as the story progresses. Is the opening of the story engaging enough to hold a reader's attention and encourage the reader to turn to page 2? Does the story reach a logical resolution, even if it is also a surprising one? Has the writing touched on all three of Aristotle's levels of persuasion: emotional, logical, and authoritative? During the feedback process the writer of the work is asked to remain quiet, take notes, and be prepared to ask questions for clarification after the discussion.

What I learned by talking to dozens of emerging military writers and writing instructors who have worked with veterans and military family members is that most military writers are apprehensive about sharing their work with the outside world. Army veteran Brooke King agrees: "The process of writing it down isn't the hardest part, it's the sharing with other people. It takes real courage to write it, but it takes real balls to open up that part of your life to complete strangers."

King says sharing military work can also be "a touchy subject" for civilian writers in a workshop. "As a society, we consciously block [war] out so that we don't have to deal with it, but for someone to come into a workshop and get a military piece critiqued is like opening up a wound again, and not everyone is receptive to the idea."

A workshop, however, is not an opportunity to defend your work to the death. I learned this the hard way. During my earliest short story workshops, when I'd fictionalized true accounts, I nearly boiled over when a fellow writer critiqued the work as completely unbelievable. Despite how true the circumstances were, I hadn't set up the scenes with adequate information to make them read credibly to my readers. In other words, I was so close to the truth that I had assumed the reader knew more than I'd allowed him or her to know. This sort of thing happens all the time to both new and experienced writers, which is why even experienced writers still rely on feedback from trusted readers before they release their work to agents and editors.

Once I peeled myself off the ceilings of those early workshops, I could see how constructive the feedback had been, and I hammered away at scene after scene until each read as 100 percent credible to my readers. And all those early essays and short stories were eventually published.

What I can't stress enough is that a writing workshop should be conducted as a judgment-free zone. I'm particularly sensitive about this detail when leading a memoir workshop. We're not there to criticize the writer's life decisions; we're there to offer feedback on the writer's *storytelling skills*. When I conduct a workshop, I insist my students provide copies of the feedback they're providing to each writer so I can ensure we're upholding our pledge to be a judgment-free workshop zone.

My favorite workshop advice for writers and instructors comes from codirector of the Queens University of Charlotte Master of Fine Arts Program, Fred Leebron, who insists that everyone offer feedback "in the manner in which they'd want it delivered to them." This Golden Rule of workshopping may seem elementary, but egos are fragile—for military veterans, including me, dare I say it, perhaps even more than others. While working on this book, I agreed to workshop a veterans writing group that meets once a month. I discovered what writing instructors had cautioned is true: military veterans, particularly older ones, aren't always open to feedback. Maybe this generalization seems unfair. The workshop I conducted included older veterans, two from World War II and the rest mostly from the Vietnam era. Only three or four had been in the Middle East wars. The younger veterans appeared more open to feedback and any advice that could make their memoirs or stories more interesting and clearer to a reader.

The older veterans, however, wanted to hear that their work was ready for publication, no matter how weak the sentence-by-sentence writing was or how underdeveloped the characters or stories might be. I'm not sure why. I can only tell you that if you want to become the best writer you can become, you'll have to open your heart and mind to constructive feedback about your work. Writers who eventually find solid publishing homes for their work understand that revision is an absolute requirement. My book-length memoir, *Eyes Right*, went through multiple drafts after various portions were workshopped and took ten years from first draft to publication release.

I have a military veteran friend who wants more than anything to write and be published, but in his rush for validation, he blitzes editors with extremely weak—usually first—drafts. He'll email for my feedback about a story, and before I can open the file, he's sent it off—warts and all—to dozens of editors, including the editor of the *New Yorker*. No surprise, his enthusiasm for writing is waning. He's burying himself under self-sabotage and the growing mountain of rejection slips. He tried writing workshops, but they didn't work for him, he told me, because he knew more than the instructor. *Seriously?*

Admittedly, writing workshops can have pitfalls. Even Stephen King in *On Writing* takes the position that workshops are largely a waste of one's time. I can't believe I'm going on the record with this, but I am: *Mr. King, I (respectfully) disagree with you . . . Sir.*

The feedback you'll receive from a writing workshop, when led by a qualified instructor, will save you countless hours of valuable writing time. Countless! You could slave away for a year on a memoir or short story and never realize what's missing within the work—and why it's being rejected by editors if you've been bold enough to submit it—because you're too close to the material or because your skills are still underdeveloped. A solid writing workshop will have pointed out the embarrassing word choice or syntax problem near the bottom of page 1; the lackluster opening paragraph that does nothing to establish a character's needs, wants, or desires; the rushed pacing of the plot; or the less-than-clear resolution.

Another welcome by-product of a writing workshop is that you're likely to learn more about how to revise your writing simply by reflecting on the feedback you and others provide one another. How much easier it is to see the flaws in someone else's writing, yes? Once you begin to notice the holes in someone else's stories—holes wide enough to drive a tank through—you'll begin to notice the holes in your own stories.

Sure, you'll learn soon enough who the workshop know-it-all is and who offers the most insightful feedback. Be wary of those who never have anything positive to say. In fact, when I'm leading a workshop, I insist that writers begin their feedback with an answer to the question *What do we like about this piece?* (or another: *What do you remember about this piece?*). I think it's important for the writer to learn what is working as much as it is to discover what's not working. We might be able to tell a new writer that we like the use of sensory language or specific details or fresh metaphors, for example, and point to specifics. We might admire another writer's use of dialogue. Another writer's strengths might be in the development of character through progressive conflicts.

Again, if you want to improve as a writer, don't dismiss the time-saving benefits of participating in a well-run writing workshop.

How do you find a writing workshop outside of a college creative writing program? Check with your local library, local college continuing education programs, and nearby va facility. Workshops designed exclusively for military veterans and their families are springing up around the country, thanks to the growing number of veterans graduating from college writing programs. Methodist University near Fort Bragg in Fayetteville, North Carolina, for example, provides a free writing workshop for veterans. The group meets one Saturday a month. Another such program is the DD-214 Veterans Writing Workshop in Tampa, Florida, which is the brainchild of Navy veteran Jeffery Hess. Hess began his veterans-only workshop in 2007. Another one, the Veterans Writing Project, is located in the Washington DC area; codirectors Ron Capps and Dario DiBattista and their fellow instructors provide free seminars and writing workshops for veterans and the families of veterans.

If a more formal writing education interests you, you could opt for a creative writing degree. After completing her undergraduate degree at Saint Leo University in Florida, Brooke King enrolled in a master of fine arts creative writing program. King was still considering law school until a creative writing workshop instructor praised her military writing. "The best writing advice I ever received was from [noted writer] Rick Moody," she said. "He told me that he had never seen a female writer, or any writer for that matter, commit to the heart-wrenching detail." When Moody discovered her plans to attend law school, he responded forcefully, encouraging her to never give up on the story, no matter how much it hurt, because, King said, "the hurt is what makes it a truly great story." King never regretted her decision to pass on law school.

After completing my bachelor's degree in creative writing in 2002, I felt I had much more to learn about the craft, so I researched graduate school creative writing programs. I wasn't in a position to move, however. When a friend mentioned that she'd stumbled across low-residency writing programs, I was intrigued and soon discovered a plethora of low-residency master of fine arts creative writing programs. A low-residency program offers the same level of academic and writing rigor but through a delivery system of online workshops with faculty and fellow student writers and with brief on-campus residencies. While some students choose an MFA program to attain college teaching credentials, most students I've encountered through the years attend an MFA program for the purpose of improving one's skills as a writer. Besides, the landscape for teaching credentials is shifting these days in favor of doctoral creative writing programs.

The bottom line is that every piece of writing can be improved. I have never participated in a workshop, including those with widely published writers, that did not include constructive feedback for everyone's work. Not one piece was perfect, if there even is such a thing. Few were even close enough to encourage the writer to submit the work to the outside world. Close perhaps but not quite there. Even writing that is eventually accepted for publication with literary journals, magazines, or publishing companies will undergo the scrutiny of editors and copyeditors.

Writing Project

JOURNAL ENTRY 23

By now you should have completed your selected military reading assignment. Pretend you're about to participate in a writing workshop that will include the author of the story you've just completed. Draft 250–500 words of feedback for this writer. Begin with: *This is a story about* _____. *What I liked most about this story is* _____. Because no story is perfect, even though this one has reached publication, record feedback for what you would recommend the writer do on the next draft. What are the overall strengths and weaknesses of the work?

Navigating the World of Publishing

Rejection slips, or form letters, however tactfully phrased, are lacerations of the soul, if not quite inventions of the devil—but there is no way around them. —ISAAC ASIMOV

When you began reading this book, you probably had an idea of how you saw yourself as a writer. Perhaps you knew a story was already inside you—maybe even your own story—and that if you could just sit down and commit it to the page, the work would one day find its way into the world and significantly affect the lives of others. Congratulations—that's what it means, in my opinion, to be an artist. Or perhaps you needed to write to regain a sense of who you were before your military service or to honor your spouse's or parent's military service or to better understand how military experience has shaped the person you've become and how it appears to be shaping your children.

Publishing, I can tell you, is both thrilling and terrifying—especially if you're publishing memoir material. I was ecstatic when the University of Nebraska Press extended an offer to publish *Eyes Right*. Soon afterward I was consumed with terror because publication meant that everyone I knew would learn about all the mistakes I'd made in the past, and they'd learn just what kind of a writer I truly was. By the publication date I was already a professor, and I worried what my colleagues would think of me as a writer. Would they think my work was good enough? Sure, you'd think that getting a book to publication should speak for itself, but it was the first time that my writing was truly out there for all to see, beyond the few short pieces I'd managed to publish in literary journals and the novel I'd published under a pseudonym.

The day *Eyes Right* was officially released, I received a 7:00 a.m. email from my mother. "Wake up, you're the lead story on AOL News." I jumped out of bed as if I'd just downed an espresso with a Red Bull chaser. Sure enough, there was a photograph—and not such a flattering one because of the enormous 1980s eyeglasses I was wearing—with the salacious headline "The Military Affair That Ended My Career." My relationship with the general was only a portion of the memoir, yet it was out there for everyone to see. I sent a text to my daughter, who was still living in Los Angeles: "Honey, I'm on AOL today." She shocked me with an immediate 4:07 a.m. Pacific Coast Time response: "I know, Dad already texted me." Her father had turned on his computer and easily recognized a photo that he had taken of me in 1980. Suddenly, there was his ex-wife under that dreadful headline.

You've heard celebrities say, "Never read the comments about stories you're in." People hiding behind "Anonymous" will write the cruelest things. The funny thing is that I actually agreed with most of the four hundred–plus negative comments. But I'd also been preparing for whatever negativity would come with the publication. I'd had years to prepare myself for what others might say or think about my story and downfall as a young Marine. My daughter, however, took the comments hard, and so did my students, who began posting comments such as: "Read the book . . . you don't know what you're talking about."

I learned something extremely valuable about myself that day: I had much thicker skin than I realized, and I had a great deal of empathy for those on the other side of the negativity. Why? I think because I had done the hard work of examining the motives behind the decisions I'd made as a Marine and, more important, the ones that had led to my downfall. I had finally found, and made, my peace.

For Brooke King the most rewarding aspect about sharing a military story is the looks she gets after telling her readers that the story they've just read, though fiction, is based largely on truth. "I cannot tell you how many people afterwards have come up to me and wanted to talk more about it. I've also had a number of vets come up and say that because I was brave enough to write it down, they, too, are going to try to commit their story to paper. That by far is my favorite part, inspiring others to write. It's why I'm a teacher and a writer. I want to encourage everyone to write. A story is only as good as what you commit to paper. If you bear your soul to your reader, your reader will feel it and be moved by your genuine humanity."

Successful writers profess that the one question they dread the most is "How do I get published?" Over the years I've heard many writers and writing instructors lament that this question is all wrong; worse yet, they say it indicates the lack of a writer's experience. You might say that asking this question is as indicative of a lack of writing experience as an opening page full of syntax and grammar mistakes.

Frankly, I thought writers who talked this way about new writers were showcasing biases, maybe even fears of seeing other writers succeed. I was wrong. In the years after completing my MFA degree and going on to teach at the university level, I, too, formed the same opinion about the writer who asks this question.

Here's the question new writers should be asking: How do I become a better writer?

Seriously. I'm not making this up. I learned this firsthand, from a workshop led by best-selling novelist Dennis Lehane. In that workshop Lehane warned against falling prey to the ticking clock syndrome. If you're at all like me, the script goes something like this: you're forty years old and should have published your first book by now—heck your fifth! Tick-tock, tick-tock. Your family is beginning to doubt this writing thing. They ask when you're going to give it all up and enjoy your life again. Tick-tock, tick-tock. Hear it?

In an inspiring foreword Lehane wrote for his agent's book, *Your First Novel: An Author Agent Team Share the Keys to Achieving Your Dream*, and shared with us during our final week of workshop, he said: "Ticking-Clock Syndrome extends beyond the point where you may or may not be ready to publish. Once the disease has taken root, it becomes a self-perpetuating virus, one that extends to all aspects of your career. You get over that first hurdle—you land an agent. Wow. An agent. But instead of enjoying it, you immediately begin wondering why that agent hasn't placed your book with a major publisher yet. I mean, it's been, like, three weeks! What are they doing up there—sipping lattes when they should be selling your book? How dare they!"

I was already forty-six that day of Lehane's workshop. I was an adjunct professor at the college—not knowing then that I'd eventually teach full-time there. I had just signed the memoir manuscript with a prestigious New York literary agency and had driven myself nearly crazy over checking email for word from my agent, so Lehane's words hit hard.

But word about the memoir manuscript dragged to months, until finally one day my agent called with this advice: write a novel instead. This was in 2006, and my agent had determined that against the plethora of war literature then being released, my experiences during the 1980s, groundbreaking though they were, weren't compelling enough.

Tick-tock, tick-tock.

I didn't know how to write a novel. My MFA degree had been in creative nonfiction. Tick-tock, tick-tock.

Disheartened though I was, I went to work on a novel. Four months later I sent the manuscript to my agent. He loved it and provided notes for revisions. Tick-tock, tick-tock.

I went back to work. Four months later I sent him the revised manuscript. He loved this one even more and sent the manuscript to editors. Weeks passed. Tick-tock, tick-tock. Eventually, everyone passed on the novel.

Editors, my agent emailed, loved the story of a woman Marine protagonist uncovering a conspiracy regarding a flawed helicopter that's dropping from the sky every other flight, but marketing didn't know how to sell military fiction to women.

His advice: write another novel.

Tick-tock, tick-tock.

So, now I had a memoir manuscript in the drawer underneath a novel manuscript.

A few weeks later I emailed the synopsis of a new novel to my agent, and the email was returned. My agent had quit the business. He hadn't bothered telling me or any of his clients, from what I would later gather. He just quit.

Quit? He *quit?*

I'm over here tick-tocking, tick-tocking, and he quit?

The more I thought about him quitting, the more determined I became. That's when I emailed the University of Nebraska Press about *Eyes Right*—for the second time in three years. You see, months before I had signed with the New York agent, I'd sent the manuscript to an editor at the University of Nebraska Press, believing that publication with such a prestigious literary press would validate me as a serious literary writer. On learning that a New York agent had offered representation, the University of Nebraska Press editor passed, believing she was doing me a favor. By the time I emailed the press a second time, it was 2010, four years after sitting in that Dennis Lehane workshop and listening to him warn us about the ticking clock syndrome. Nebraska's editor read the new version of the memoir, which by then was at least the fifth revision since she'd read the 2005 version. This time Nebraska wanted the memoir. I'll never forget that day in Florida when I read the email from the editor. My first reaction, looking back, seems both strange and expected. I remember saying to my new husband, "Now what was so hard about that?" The memoir had finally found a home and the best one possible. Had my agent not quit, I would never have become determined enough to take control of my own writing career.

As writers are fond of saying, "Good work will always find its way into the world." I believe this, too, but I also know a great number of writers whose excellent work has yet to make it into the world. I see and hear their desperation. I can't explain why some work makes it faster into the world than other good work. I can only tell you that the path to publication for me happened at the best possible moment in my life. For starters I was in a healthier marriage. In

2005, when I signed the memoir with the New York agent, my third husband had broken the jubilant atmosphere by declaring, "If you think I'm going to become Mrs. Tracy Crow, you can think again." I was stunned. I went to bed that night praying that the book wouldn't sell, for how could I consciously choose a book over my marriage? Hadn't I learned anything from my previous mistakes about putting career before marriage?

Every published writer has a story about that first book. Some writers appear like overnight successes when in actuality they've been writing and publishing, as did I, in literary journals for years, honing craft and attending writing workshops. Suddenly, it seems, they are the Next Big Thing.

In his book *Outliers: The Story of Success* Malcolm Gladwell asserts that to become truly proficient at something, we must be willing to devote roughly ten thousand hours toward the study of it. Ten thousand hours is about ten years. Or broken down further, about two and a half hours a day for ten years. I didn't write every day for two and a half hours, but I started seriously writing in 2002, and my first book was published ten years later, in 2012.

What's my advice? *Don't quit.* But realize that nobody is really going to care about whether you ever publish an essay, short story, or book, so if you're determined to get your work into the world, you will have to put in the work—maybe even as many as ten thousand hours—and learn what you can about the craft and business side of publishing.

After years and years of traditional publishing models, the business of publishing is rapidly changing, thanks to electronic book markets that include Nook, Kindle, and iPad. Today writers have more choices than ever about how their work will be delivered to their readers.

The traditional model of publishing requires a writer to query literary agents, who are now the true editors and gatekeepers of the publishing world, for agents are the ones who spend countless hours helping their stable of writers to massage a manuscript for a particular editor of a large publishing house. (At the end of this book I've included a copy of the query letter that I used in the body of an email during my agent search. I've shared the letter with many others to use as a template, and they've also found success with this model.)

Agents have their ear to the ground of publishing. They know which editors at various publishing houses are eager to sign the next great vampire series writer and who is willing to consider a provocative military novel or memoir. Agents know not to waste their time on editors who would never have an interest in a military story. So, agents are crucial if you're determined to follow the traditional path of publishing. On this path a new writer can generally expect an advance, though advances in recent years have considerably dwindled. Dwindling advances are not necessarily a bad thing because advances must be earned out in sales; a huge advance that doesn't earn out in sales will most likely sour a publisher toward your second book.

The traditional publishing route also includes university presses, such as the one publishing this book, and small independent presses. These presses typically don't pay advances, but they deliver an unmistakable level of literary prestige.

Let's say you've found an agent and your agent has sold your book to a traditional publisher, large or small. Expect eighteen months to two years before the release of the book. Within the first six months or so of the purchase, you'll eventually receive editing notes for revisions. You'll have about six months or so to make those revisions. Afterward the book goes through a copyediting process and back to you again for approval, comments, and revisions. Meanwhile, marketing is looking over the AIF (author information form) that you were asked to complete. The AIF includes your thoughts about such things as who you think your readers are and what titles on the market are similar to yours.

If you're lucky, you'll be allowed to provide input regarding the cover image for your book. Few writers get more than a little input. When the University of Nebraska Press asked for my input on *Eyes Right*, I sent a dozen or so images that reflected what I saw within the book as deeply brooding or provocative themes regarding self-change. Nebraska sent back a bright aqua cover with a faceless paper doll image. I wasn't sold, but I'd learned from other writers that it's best to allow marketing to do what marketing does best. I sweated about that cover for a year. Turns out, marketing at Nebraska was genius. The cover has been a huge hit among readers and is inviting to women without any military experiences. Unless you're Stephen King, you're not likely to get much control over your cover image, or even over your title. Some things you just have to let go of and trust the experts.

In the nontraditional model of publishing, the writer bypasses the agent/editor model, uploading a properly formatted manuscript to an on-demand and ebook publisher. Amazon (Kindle) and Barnes & Noble (Nook) make it extremely easy for writers to upload their books. You'll still need an arresting cover image, and you might even have to pay for it, so there are some costs associated with the nontraditional method. I tell writers to expect to spend five hundred to a thousand dollars to publish an ebook, though many writers spend far less.

Writing Project

JOURNAL ENTRY 24

What changes in perspective have you noticed from the beginning of your journal entries to this final entry? What assumptions about writing—or about yourself as a writer or about military writing—have been supported or challenged?

JOURNAL ENTRY 25

Review your definition of writing success from Journal Entry 3. In what ways has your definition of success been supported or altered? How would you define writing success for yourself now?

JOURNAL ENTRY 26

And finally, in what ways have your sense of self and your sense of your place in the world been shaped or altered throughout this *On Point* writing and reading project?

10

Gifting Ourselves with a Writing Life

It's hard to decide who's truly brilliant; it's easier to see who's driven, which in the long run may be more important. —MICHAEL CRICHTON, CONGO

Years ago, after mailing off the Carver Greene novel manuscript to my agent, I joined my third husband (now ex-husband) in the living room for a mini-celebration. "It's done," I said, and danced across the hardwood floors before sinking onto the leather sofa. My husband, stony-faced, sat still across the room. "What's wrong?" I said.

"I've decided to go back to school." He was sixty-four and twenty-one years my senior. Although he had reached financial success as a business entrepreneur—even selling his business for a sum he never thought he'd see in his lifetime—the idea that I had recently completed bachelor and graduate degrees in creative writing had been bothering him more than I allowed myself to consider. Retirement in Florida hadn't been the paradise he'd hoped for. His facelift a year earlier hadn't provided the ego boost he'd expected. He was bored. He had never developed interests outside of building businesses, and since those years were receding as fast as his hairline, he was growing more and more restless. He had been talking lately and often about living abroad as an expat in Costa Rica or Panama. I was all for life in another country, for I saw the whole thing as an adventure that would lead to rich writing material. Now he wanted to finish college.

"I think going back to school is a wonderful idea," I said. Because we walked four miles on the beach around sunset every evening, I was already predicting the insightful talks we'd have about what he was learning. "What are you thinking of majoring in?"

"Creative writing," he said, and appeared to be waiting for a reaction before adding, "I plan to major in creative writing to prove to you that anybody could have written *Jurassic Park*." To this day I have no idea why he chose *Jurassic Park* as his target. Sorry, Michael Crichton.

Amazing how many thoughts, or fragments of thoughts, the mind can dispatch in the time it takes to blink. I first witnessed this when a drunk driver came over a hill on the interstate one evening and struck my car head-on. I was driving. I had barely the time to blurt, "Oh my god!" when *bam!* But that didn't stop my mind from being flooded with thoughts about how my father had died in a fiery car crash just two months before my first wedding and wondering if I was thinking about him now because he was in the car with me to save me or to take me to the other side, and so on, and so on . . . all within the time it took me to shriek, "Oh my god!" followed by the *bam!*

So, that day in the living room, in the split seconds that followed my husband's *Jurassic Park* comment, I realized I was witnessing the end of our marriage. I was floating above the room and saw myself rise from the leather sofa, reach for my purse and keys that I'd dropped in a nearby chair, and drive off into the unknown.

But then empathy for the man sitting across the room flooded me. He was obviously hurting so much—self-induced hurting, as it was—that he felt the need to prove that he, too, could write, would write, would write better than I ever dreamed of writing, because, after all, anyone could have written *Jurassic Park*.

I didn't walk out. Instead, I encouraged him. Who was I to steal another's dream of writing when I had dreamed of becoming a writer since I was ten?

Within a few days he was enrolled in the local college's continuing education program. He started his first writing class and completed his first short memoir. In no time we filled our four-mile beach walks with discussions about the writers he was reading for classes and the writing techniques he was applying toward short memoir pieces. By then I was teaching creative writing at a nearby university. Occasionally, my husband would ask me to look over a paragraph or two, and I was super-impressed with his storytelling voice.

But eight courses later he announced he was quitting.

Quitting college.

Quitting writing.

Quitting our marriage.

He was moving to Costa Rica, alone. Writing was too hard, he said and added that he couldn't bear the thought that I was a better writer.

"But you're just getting started," I heard myself plead, as if to one of my college freshmen. "Give yourself more time." But I knew it was over, and for a moment I was sadder that the world would miss out on his writing voice than what I would miss about our marriage.

I'm telling you all this now to warn you that when we grow and blossom into even better versions of ourselves, those around us sometimes feel as if they're withering in the shadow of our growth. Losing my marriage taught me that each of us has a path to walk, demons to overcome, and possibly regrets to face. For a while I struggled to reclaim my writing. When I couldn't write, I read.

When I did start writing again, I was rewarded with publications in some of the country's most prestigious literary journals, with writing awards and recognition, and with teaching offers. As nineteenth-century poet Emily Dickinson wrote, "A wounded deer leaps the highest."

Here's the harsh bottom line . . . nobody died. Nobody died because my now ex-husband decided to give up his writing just as he was becoming a more artful writer. And nobody will die if you and I decide to quit.

I hope you won't quit.

Now that you've given yourself this gift of time to explore the concept of writing about your military experiences—whether you're writing them down as memoir or fiction or for your eyes only—I hope you continue to gift yourself with a writing, self-examined life.

Will the work be hard at times? Of course. If everyone could write a compelling military story, everyone would. But not everyone can. If you've made it this far in *On Point*, I dare say you can and will.

My hope is that you'll go on to write many stories about your military experiences and eventually write on all sorts of topics and across several genres. David Abrams believes writing is a mind-set: "I never thought of myself as a military writer, but rather as a writer who happened to be in the military."

So, keep writing, and keep growing as a writer. Honor the rituals that feed and nurture your writing life. *On Point* is not the end of your discovery about becoming a writer and inhabiting a writing life. *On Point* is just a beginning.

Additional Resources

Recommended Military Reading

All Quiet on the Western Front by Erich Maria Remarque (novel—World War I)

Anabasis by Xenophon (autobiographical—ancient wars)

The Backwash of War as Witnessed by an American Nurse by Ellen LaMotte (memoir—World War I)

The Balkan Express by Slavenka Drakulić (essays—Bosnia-Herzegovina)

Band of Sisters: American Women at War in Iraq by Kirsten Holmstedt (nonfiction—Iraq)

Buffalo Soldiers by Robert O'Connor (novel—1960s era)

Burning the Days: Recollection by James Salter (memoir—Korea)

Catch-22 by Joseph Heller (novel—World War II)

Ceremony by Leslie Marmon Silko (novel—Korea)

Chickenhawk by Robert Mason (memoir—Vietnam)

Civil War Stories by Ambrose Bierce (short stories—Civil War)

Dispatches by Michael Herr (novel—Vietnam)

Dog Soldiers by Robert Stone (novel—Vietnam)

Eyes Right: Confessions from a Woman Marine by Tracy Crow (memoir—Cold War era)

A Farewell to Arms by Ernest Hemingway (novel—World War I)

The Final Salute by Kathleen M. Rodgers (novel—Middle East)

Flashman by George MacDonald Fraser (novel—British wars)

Fobbit by David Abrams (novel—Iraq)

For Love of Country: What Our Veterans Can Teach Us about Citizenship, Heroism, and Sacrifice by Howard Schultz and Rajiv Chandrasekaran (biography—Afghanistan, Iraq)

For Whom the Bell Tolls by Ernest Hemingway (novel—Spanish Civil War)

The Gallic Wars by Julius Caesar (memoir)

Generation Kill by Evan Wright (nonfiction—Iraq)

Going after Cacciato by Tim O'Brien (novel—Vietnam)

Gone to Soldiers by Marge Piercy (novel—World War II)

Here, Bullet by Brian Turner (poetry—Iraq)

Hesitation Kills: A Female Officer's Combat Experience in Iraq by Jane Blair (memoir—Iraq)

Home before Morning: The Story of an Army Nurse in Vietnam by Lynda Van Devanter (memoir—Vietnam)

Home of the Brave, vols. 1–2 edited by Jeffery Hess (fiction anthology—vol. 1: World War II to present; vol. 2: Middle East wars)

The Hunters by James Salter (novel—Korea)

The Iliad by Homer (ancient Greek poem—Trojan War)

In Country by Bobbie Ann Mason (novel—Vietnam)

In Pharaoh's Army by Tobias Wolff (memoir—Vietnam)

It Happened on the Way to War by Rye Barcott (memoir—Iraq, Bosnia, Horn of Africa)

Jarhead: A Marine's Chronicle of the Gulf War by Anthony Swofford (memoir—Gulf War)

Johnny Got His Gun by Dalton Trumbo (memoir—World War I)

The Last True Story I'll Ever Tell by John Crawford (memoir—Iraq)

Living with Honor: A Memoir by Medal of Honor Recipient Staff Sergeant Salvatore A. Giunta by Sal Giunta and Joe Layden (memoir—Afghanistan)

The Long Walk by Brian Castner (memoir—Iraq)

Losing Tim by Janet Burroway (memoir—Iraq)

Love My Rifle More than You: Young and Female in the U.S. Army by Kayla Williams (memoir—Iraq)

Man's Search for Meaning by Viktor Frankl (memoir—World War II)

Matterhorn by Karl Marlantes (novel—Vietnam)

Meditations in Green by Stephen Wright (novel—Vietnam)

My Departure: A Memoir by Tracy Kidder (memoir—Vietnam War)

My Life as a Foreign Country by Brian Turner (memoir—Iraq, Afghanistan, Bosnia)

My War: Killing Time in Iraq by Colby Buzzell (memoir—Iraq)

The Naked and the Dead by Norman Mailer (novel—World War II)

No-No Boy by John Okada (World War II)

Obscenities by Michael Casey (poetry—Vietnam)

Paco's Story by Larry Heinemann (novel—Vietnam)

Red, White, and True: Stories from Veterans and Their Families, World War II to Present edited by Tracy Crow (nonfiction—various wars)

The Red Badge of Courage by Stephen Crane (novel—Civil War)

Red Earth: A Vietnam Warrior's Journey by Philip H. Red Eagle (memoir—Vietnam)

Refresh, Refresh by Benjamin Percy (short stories—Iraq)

A Rumor of War by Philip Caputo (novel—Vietnam)

S by Slavenka Drakulić (novel—Bosnia-Herzegovina)

Seriously Not All Right: Five Wars in Ten Years by Ron Capps (memoir—Iraq, Afghanistan, Kosovo, and others)

Slaughterhouse-Five by Kurt Vonnegut (novel—World War II)

Sniper by Charles Henderson (biography—Vietnam)

The Things They Carried by Tim O'Brien (novel—Vietnam)

The Thin Red Line by James Jones (novel—World War II)

Three Guineas by Virginia Woolf (essays—World War I)

Three Soldiers by John Dos Passos (novel—World War I)

Uncommon Valor: The Medal of Honor and the Warriors Who Earned It in Afghanistan and Iraq by Dwight Jon Zimmerman and John D. Gresham (biography—Afghanistan, Iraq)

An Unlawful Order by Carver Greene (Tracy Crow's pen name) (novel—Afghanistan, Iraq)

What It Is Like to Go to War by Karl Marlantes (essay—Vietnam)

When Heaven and Earth Changed Places by Le Ly Hayslip (novel—Vietnam)

When We Walked above the Clouds: A Memoir of Vietnam by H. Lee Barnes (memoir—Vietnam)

Woman in Amber: Healing the Trauma of War by Agate Nesaule (memoir—World War II)

The Yellow Birds by Kevin Powers (novel—Iraq)

You Know When the Men Are Gone by Siobhan Fallon (short stories—Iraq)

My Favorite Writing Craft Books

Bird by Bird: Some Instructions on Writing and Life by Anne Lamott

Braving the Fire: A Guide to Writing about Grief and Loss by Jessica Handler

Eats, Shoots, and Leaves: The Zero Tolerance Approach to Punctuation by Lynne Truss

The Elements of Style by William Strunk and E. B. White

Good Prose: The Art of Nonfiction by Tracy Kidder and Richard Todd

Making a Good Script Great by Linda Seger

On Becoming a Novelist by John Gardner

On Writing: A Memoir of the Craft by Stephen King

Reading like a Writer: A Guide for People Who Love Books and for Those Who Want to Write Them by Francine Prose

Story: Substance, Structure, Style, and the Principles of Screenwriting by Robert McKee

Three Genres: The Writing of Fiction / Literary Nonfiction, Poetry, and Drama by Stephen Minot

Word Painting and *Write Your Heart Out* by Rebecca McClanahan

Writing Fiction: A Guide to Narrative Craft and *Imaginative Writing* by Janet Burroway

Resources for the Military Community

Defense Centers of Excellence for Psychological Health and Traumatic Brain Injury's 24/7 live chat outreach center: 1-866-966-1020, or email resources@dcoeoutreach.org

Moral Injury Healing: http://projects.huffingtonpost.com/moral-injury /healing

Operation Homecoming: Writing the Wartime Experience (documentary, 80 mins.)

The Pass in Review: http://www.amazon.com/The-Pass-In-ReviewVolume/dp /149602835X/ref=tmm_pap_title_0?ie=UTF8&qid=1393715741&sr=8-1

Pentagon website Military OneSource for short-term, nonmedical counseling

Student Veterans of America: http://www.studentveterans.org/

Veterans Crisis Line: 1-800-273-8255

Veterans Writing Project: http://veteranswriting.org/ and http://o-dark -thirty.org/

Warrior Writers Project: http://www.warriorwriters.org/about.html

Wounded Warrior Project: http://www.woundedwarriorproject.org/

Wounded Warrior Regiment: DoD CAP (Computer/Electronic Accommodations Program) for assistive devices in computers, talking dictionaries, and other accommodations, http://www.woundedwarriorregiment.org /wwr/assets/File/FactSheets/ComputerAccommodatioProgramSlick Sheet.pdf

A Few Writing Shortcut Tips

- Avoid opening your story with a line of dialogue. The reader has no context for the speaker and will have to reread the dialogue after the introduction has finally been made.
- Consider a fresher story opening than the weather.
- Eliminate the use of anything other than said for most dialogue tags.
- Remember to incorporate sensory language that appeals to the five senses: sight, touch, smell, sound, and taste.
- Review Kurt Vonnegut's "Eight Basics of Creative Writing." Often. Enough said.
- Remember that without conflict there is no story worth telling.
- Drop your reader in media res (in the middle of a conflict) to stir curiosity about your character's needs, wants, goals, and desires.
- Consider the industry "one-page rule" of establishing conflict and/or interesting characters for your reader: if the reader (agent or editor) isn't hooked by the end of page 1, the reader might not turn to page 2.
- Brush up on grammar. Nothing screams amateurish more than a manuscript that's riddled with grammar and syntax problems.
- Don't be afraid to use contractions, especially in dialogue. Don't most of us speak with contractions?
- Look at a few scenes and determine the opening and closing energy. Does the energy change from beginning to end?
- Establish rituals and habits with regard to time of day and location for your best writing experience. Cherish that which nurtures your writing life.
- Employ the writer's adage of "Show, don't tell," a reminder that character is revealed through scenes with actions and dialogue. A better adage, however, is "Show and tell": remember to reveal the internal conflicts, the motives and intentions, that fuel a character's choice under conflict.
- Seek a writing workshop that includes an instructor with teaching and publishing experience.
- Read. Read. Read.
- Write. Write. Write.

Tracy's Sample Email Query Letter for Agents

Dear _____

I'm seeking representation for my 63,000-word memoir manuscript, "Eyes Right," about my life as a woman Marine during the groundbreaking 1980s.

Before the Jessica Lynches and Shoshanna Johnsons fought in the deserts of the Middle East, my generation was fighting gender bias and personal fears of failure here, on American soil. As an award-winning military journalist, I experienced a great deal more than the average Marine.

By way of a brief introduction, my recent literary nonfiction has appeared in the *Missouri Review, Mississippi Review, Puerto del Sol,* and *Literary Mama,* among others. Three essays were nominated for Pushcart Prizes. I have an MFA in creative writing and teach journalism and writing at the University of Tampa in Florida.

Two excerpts from "Eyes Right" have recently been published. Editor Monica Torres of *Puerto del Sol* states in her acceptance letter that her readers appreciated "the candor, the details and straightforward prose of the piece, as well as the insights they gleaned about life for a military woman who was also a wife and mother"—material Monica states her readers called "timely and fresh."

Editor Shari McDonald of *Literary Mama* refers to the excerpt she published as "so gorgeous, so rich, so descriptive . . . it's phenomenal and one of my favorites."

"Eyes Right" is for any woman in a leadership position today who fears she cannot recover after failure. While primarily a coming-of-age story, I also explore and examine motives that compelled me to break the cycle of alcoholism within my family and those that drove me toward success at the expense of my marriage and ultimately my career.

When an affair I had with a prominent general was discovered—the general and I threatened with a court-martial—I fell on the sword, saving the general, my family, and the Marine Corps from public embarrassment.

Below you will find early blurbs for "Eyes Right." I look forward to hearing from you.

All best,
Tracy Crow